THE CRUSADERS

THE
CRUSADERS

Norman Housley

TEMPUS

First published 2002

PUBLISHED IN THE UNITED KINGDOM BY:
Tempus Publishing Ltd
The Mill, Brimscombe Port
Stroud, Gloucestershire GL5 2QG

PUBLISHED IN THE UNITED STATES OF AMERICA BY:
Tempus Publishing Inc.
2 Cumberland Street
Charleston, SC 29401

British Library Cataloguing in Publication Data.
A catalogue record for this book is available from the British Library.

ISBN 0 7524 2554 4

Typesetting and origination by Tempus Publishing.
PRINTED AND BOUND IN THE USA.

CONTENTS

For Viv, Bill, Emma, Jenny and Charlotte

PREFACE

In a statement issued on 24 September 2001 Osama bin Laden described the allied troops who were fighting in Afghanistan as 'the new Jewish and Christian Crusader campaign that is led by the Chief Crusader Bush under the banner of the Cross'. It is a very long time since relations between the Islamic and Western worlds have been as tense as they are today, and a recurrent theme in Islamic suspicions of the West is that of a new Crusade. Clearly the time is ripe to pose fundamental questions about the original Crusaders. Who were they? What were they fighting for? How did they perceive themselves and their enemies?

My aim in this book is to allow the answers to such questions to emerge through the writings of the Crusaders themselves. Basing my argument on four classic texts written by and about Crusaders, and ranging from the time of the First Crusade to the early fifteenth century, I have tried to build up a convincing picture of Crusader psychology. Throughout I have focused on the central conundrum of the crusading experience: wars which were waged in the name of the Prince of Peace by individuals who wore the most poignant symbol of Christ's self-sacrifice.

I am grateful to Jonathan Reeve of Tempus Publishing for suggesting that I write this book, and to Viv Prescot and Jonathan Riley-Smith for reading it in draft.

Norman Housley
May 2002

1

THE 'GESTA FRANCORUM' AND THE FIRST CRUSADE:

PILGRIMS IN ARMS

In September 1187, following his massive victory over the Frankish army at Hattin, the Sultan Saladin laid siege to Jerusalem. According to the chronicler Ibn al-Athir, a request from the besieged that they should be allowed to surrender the city in exchange for their lives met with a bitter response:

> 'We shall deal with you just as you dealt with the population of Jerusalem when you took it in 1099, with murder and enslavement and other such savageries'.

The Frankish commander in Jerusalem pointed out that such an approach would not only cause the defenders to fight to the last man but also provoke them to pull down the most holy Muslim shrines, the mosque of Omar (Dome of the Rock) and the al-Aqsa mosque (Solomon's Palace). Saladin quickly changed tack and allowed the Franks in Jerusalem to ransom themselves. But his initial reply was telling: it showed how fully the terrible events of July 1099 (when the first Crusaders stormed Jerusalem) had become lodged in the collective memory of the Islamic world. Nor did it end there. In his Dimbleby lecture of December 2001 former US President Bill Clinton referred to the massacre which took place in July 1099 as 'a travesty that is still being discussed today in the Middle East'. He may well have been countering statements recently made by Osama bin Laden that stigmatized the US assault on Taliban forces in Afghanistan as a new Crusade. Bin Laden's statement of 24 September 2001, for example, made no fewer than five references to crusading. The al-Qaʻeda leader did not single out the First Crusade for comment but it has always been at the forefront of Islamic resentment of crusading, not just because of the culminating massacre in Jerusalem but also because it established a Catholic presence in the Middle East which lasted nearly 200 years.

For Muslims, Western leaders and Christians today seeking to explain the on-going turmoil of the Middle East, the first Crusaders were guilty men. To their contemporaries in Western Europe things looked very different. Jerusalem had been conquered by the Arabs in 638 and its recapture by Christians after more than four centuries was regarded as miraculous. For the Benedictine monk and chronicler Robert of Reims, writing in the first decade of the twelfth century, the First Crusade was an example of divine intervention which could be compared only with the creation of the world and with Christ's redemption of mankind through his death on the Cross. We have to resist the temptation to dismiss such comments as triumphalist rhetoric or excited hyperbole. For Catholics living in the early twelfth century, what had been achieved by the first Crusaders, the 'Jerusalemites' as they became known, gave a cast-iron certainty to the justice and holiness of their cause. Their battle cry, 'deus vult', 'God wills it', had been confirmed by success. In the course of their march of some 4,300 km from Western Europe to Palestine, involving three years in the field, they had fought several pitched battles and conducted numerous sieges. They had endured a series of famines, the last so disastrous that some Crusaders resorted to cannibalism. Rivalry amongst the leaders had brought the Crusade close to breaking up and many Crusaders had become so demoralized that they deserted, despite the personal and family shame involved and the contempt with which they knew they would be greeted at home. Who could seriously doubt that the hand of God was present?

Robert of Reims was one of three Benedictine monks living in northern France who wrote histories of the Crusade in the early 1100s; the others were Baldric of Bourgueil and Guibert of Nogent (the most famous). There is naturally a danger that narratives written by educated and cloistered monks, who had not been on the Crusade themselves and who were concerned above all to give it a theological interpretation, would distort beyond all recognition the motives and attitudes of the participants. And this is precisely where our text comes to the rescue. Robert, Baldric and Guibert all wrote that they had read a narrative account of the Crusade, which dissatisfied them in part because it was written in very plain Latin. This text was the 'Deeds of the Franks and the others going to Jerusalem' (*Gesta Francorum et aliorum Hierosolimitanorum*, hereafter GF). The GF was completed very shortly after the fall of Jerusalem, perhaps in 1099; most of it was probably written during the campaign itself. We do not know the name of its author, usually called the 'Anonymous', who was either a knight or a cleric. He was a Norman, a follower of Bohemond Prince of Taranto, one of the ambitious Norman warlords who in the late eleventh century were engaged in constructing military lordships amidst the political debris of southern Italy. In the last stage of the Crusade Bohemond stayed in the captured city of Antioch instead of proceeding southward to Jerusalem, and the 'Anonymous' left his service. But when Bohemond sailed back to France in 1106 to secure the support of Pope Paschal II for a new Crusade which would help him to consolidate his position at Antioch, he took with him copies of the GF; most of it was highly complimentary to Bohemond and would help him argue his cause. This brought the GF to the disapproving attention of Robert, Baldric and Guibert, whose own accounts of the First Crusade were much more elaborate. But it also assisted the survival of a text which otherwise might never have made its way beyond Jerusalem's walls.

In the GF, then, we possess a full description of the First Crusade, almost 100 pages long, which was written by a participant during and very shortly after the expedition. Its author did not have access to the counsels of the leaders (*seniores*) and he tells us very little about their manoeuvrings, but if we are outside the tents where the deals were struck, we are in the battle lines and on the walls of the castles and towns. No single source can give us an insight into the thinking of all the first Crusaders. But the GF comes as close as we can hope to communicating their thought and behaviour, the religious hopes and convictions which drove them onward, and the social habits and military techniques which they fell back on and skilfully adapted to achieve success.

One reason why Robert of Reims found the GF unsatisfactory was its very off-hand treatment of the origins of the First Crusade: 'it contained no

1. Bohemond of Taranto's elaborate tomb, Canosa, Apulia.

description of the foundation of the Crusade at the council of Clermont'. It is true that the call to Crusade, which Pope Urban II made at Clermont in the Auvergne on 27 November 1095 – without doubt one of the most important sermons ever preached – was encapsulated in a few phrases, whereas other histories of the First Crusade reproduced what they claimed to be Urban's full text. This is not a great disadvantage. A relatively small percentage of those who took the Cross in 1095–6 had actually heard Urban II speak. Most probably responded to itinerant preachers, who gave their own twist to what the Pope had said, and of course the Crusaders' own understanding of what they heard differed from person to person. Nevertheless, the First Crusade would not have occurred without the Clermont sermon, thus many attempts have been made to establish the gist of Urban's message. The sources are not helpful. The official decree, the council's minute as it were, is notoriously laconic: 'Whoever for devotion only, not to gain honour or money, goes to Jerusalem to liberate the Church of God can substitute this journey for all penance.' In other words, the Pope preached a war of liberation, which was simultaneously a devotional exercise, a variant of pilgrimage; if it was carried out for the right reasons, it would earn its participants forgiveness for all their sins. Yet these brief phrases carry a heavy freight of ambiguity. This is especially true of the 'Church of God' and the place of the city of Jerusalem in Urban's thinking.

The Pope was of course primarily hoping for the recovery of Jerusalem's shrines, above all the church of the Holy Sepulchre. The Emperor Constantine had constructed a magnificent basilica in the north-western quarter of Jerusalem, around what was believed, following excavations in 325/6, to be the tomb of Christ. On the command of the Fatimid caliph al-Hakim, this church was largely destroyed, together with the tomb itself, in 1009. In 1036–40 the Byzantine Emperor Michael IV Paphlagon rebuilt the tomb, surrounding it with a galleried rotunda. This modest construction had become Christendom's most revered shrine. But for a pope in 1095 the 'Church of God' was bound to have a broader resonance. We know from letters which Urban wrote shortly after he preached at Clermont that he saw the Crusade as part of a pattern of Christian defence and recovery which included, most notably, the recent advances made in Spain against the Moors. And the sermon at Clermont was probably triggered by Urban II's reception of an embassy from the Emperor of Constantinople, Alexius I Comnenus. Alexius requested Western assistance to drive the Turks out of the Byzantine lands in Asia Minor, which they had conquered in the 1070s. It was not just sacred shrines which were to be liberated in the East, but fellow-Christians, even those whose beliefs and rites were suspiciously different from those held and practised by Catholics.

Urban's activities and letters in the months after the council of Clermont give a strong impression of a forceful man making every effort to give shape to the Crusade and to maintain some form of control over it. The range of Urban's ambition cannot be faulted. He tried to bar monks from going and limit recruitment for the Crusade to fighting men. He attempted to exclude Spanish knights because their services were needed at home in the struggle against the Moors. It is possible that he entertained hopes that the Crusade would increase the level of peace existing within Western Europe because trouble-makers would go on Crusade and be converted by the experience. Few of these plans worked in practice. Recruitment for the Crusade could not be controlled. Its appeal knew no geographical or social limits; Scots fought in the same army as Normans from southern Italy and knights marched with peasants. All the sources for the Crusade testify to the breadth, the catholicity, of its attraction. And as one would expect, the departure of many great lords on the Crusade caused, rather than solving, problems of local order, while those trouble-makers that did go had no qualms about resuming their old habits when they returned.

Whether Urban II had a real comprehension of the force he had unleashed is questionable. It is unlikely that he had a blueprint for what should be done once Jerusalem was in Christian hands. But he certainly created the idea, which resided at the heart of the Crusade's appeal: the fusion of warfare and devotion in 'armed pilgrimage'. The *GF* makes crystal clear both the revolutionary nature of this synthesis and its impact. The Crusade came to Bohemond's attention when he was besieging Amalfi; he received news that 'a huge host of Christians had arrived, Franks journeying to the Holy Sepulchre and ready to fight against the pagans'. Bohemond made inquiries about their weaponry, their insignia and their battle cry. The answers were that they were well-armed, that they displayed Christ's Cross on their right arm or on their chest, and that their battle cry was a repeated shout of 'God wills it' ('deus vult'). Bohemond was 'inspired by the Holy Spirit': he resolved to join the Crusade and ordered his most valuable cloak to be cut up into crosses for all who wished to come with him. The passage is artful, emphasizing Bohemond's piety and enthusiasm, but it does pinpoint with some precision what was startlingly new about this army. These were pilgrims in arms, people engaged in one of the oldest devotional activities known to Christians but also equipped for warfare. They wore a cloth Cross as a symbol of their determination to carry our Christ's command in

Matthew 16:24, which was quoted at the very start of the *GF*: 'if any man will come after me, let him deny himself, and take up his Cross, and follow me.' And their battle cry was not the name of a lord, a castle or a saint, but an invocation of God's authority, which lay behind the Crusade and was mediated through his lieutenant on earth, the Pope.

In one respect it is not hard to appreciate the appeal of the Crusade, the guarantee of full forgiveness of sins to those who completed this single penitential exercise had never been made before and this alone must have electrified audiences wherever the Crusade was preached. During the preaching of the Second Crusade St Bernard of Clairvaux would characterize it as an offer simply too good to refuse. Other aspects of crusading's appeal are less immediately comprehensible; they were more closely attuned to the peculiarities of Western European, and especially French, society as it had developed by the end of the eleventh century. In the first place, pilgrimage was probably the most popular of all the devotional practices open to the laity and many people who took the Cross in 1095–6 would have been on at least one pilgrimage before, if not to one of the great centres (Jerusalem, Rome and Santiago), then to one or more of Europe's plethora of regional shrine churches. It used to be thought that the Crusade was a response to the disruption of the pilgrim route to Jerusalem caused by the occupation of Palestine by the Seljuq Turks in the second half of the eleventh century. There had certainly been considerable turmoil when the Turks, who were Sunni Muslims, reached the limits of a great westward thrust which originated south of the Aral Sea, and drove their Shi'i rivals of the Fatimid dynasty from Syria and Palestine. The Turks seized Jerusalem in 1071 and held it continuously, after a brief Fatimid recovery, from 1076 onward. But this sequence of events does not fit the chronology of the Crusade. For while it remained dangerous to cross Anatolia (Asia Minor) and Syria, there was no serious fighting in Palestine after 1076.

What had changed were less external circumstances in the East than religious sensibilities in the West. Increasingly the occupation of Jerusalem by Muslims was viewed as a source of pollution to its religious shrines. To Catholic Christians, of course, this was true irrespective of whether the Muslims were Sunni Turks or Shi'i Fatimids. Baldric of Bourgueil, for example, described Urban II in his Clermont sermon lamenting the neglect or ill-treatment of three of the great shrines: the abbey-church of St Mary in the valley of Jehoshaphat, the Temple of Solomon (the Dome of the Rock), and the church of the Holy Sepulchre. But it was not just the shrines which were suffering: the whole region where Christ had lived, taught and

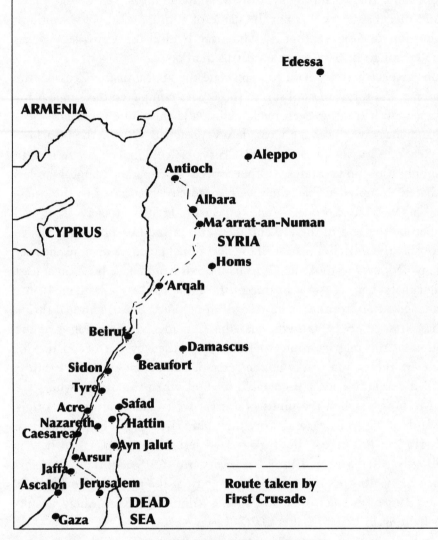

2. Palestine and Syria, 1095–1291.

preached was sacred ground. As Baldric states that Urban went on to remark, 'this land we have deservedly called holy in which there is not even a foot-step that the body or spirit of the Saviour did not render glorious and blessed'. All of Palestine comprised *terra sancta* – the Holy Land.

The two-fold tendency to regard certain defined spaces as holy and to lay stress on Christ's humanity benefited the Holy Land more than it did anywhere else. But other important trends in religious thinking in this period also worked to Jerusalem's advantage. One was eschatology, the belief that all historical events were part of God's preordained plan for the conversion of gentiles and the salvation of believers. Jerusalem was central to the eschatological world view, and the belief that geographically it lay at the centre of the world underpinned this view. 'The navel of the world' as Robert of Reims put it, the city was the birthplace of the Christian religion, and it was destined to be the site of Christ's return and of the Last Judgement. Clearly it must be in Christian hands for these events. Prophecies that the Last Days were imminent became widespread at the time of the preaching of the Crusade. There were outbreaks of ergotism ('holy fire'), an epidemic caused by eating bread made from mouldy rye, which in the past had given rise to mass pilgrimages. And there was a remarkable sequence of natural phenomena, which led some contemporaries to believe that a crisis in history was at hand, including a meteor shower in April 1095 and eclipses of the moon in February and August 1096.

Part of Jerusalem's magnetic appeal derived from its multiplicity of symbolic roles. If the most popular one was that it prefigured heaven, there was also the idea that the city represented the Church, and Catholic unity was fractured without control over it. The Muslim occupation was particularly shameful for Catholic Christendom because by 1095 it had a powerful sense of its own identity. Contemporaries made much of the fact that the Crusaders spoke different languages, revealing their destination in communities which they passed through by making the sign of the Cross with their fingers. But they shared a liturgical language in which Jerusalem, whatever the precise shade of meaning attached to the word, occurred repeatedly. The Holy Land had come to exercise a claim on the spiritual allegiance of Catholics, which complemented their common acceptance of the doctrinal supremacy (*magisterium*) of the papacy and the liturgical rites of the Roman Church. That claim could not be ignored: Robert of Reims portrayed Jerusalem physically calling to the West to be liberated from the Muslims.

It would be hard to exaggerate the degree to which the devotional and, in particular, the ascetic practices which had formed around Catholic pilgrimage shaped the religious outlook of the early Crusaders. It was not until the late twelfth century that the Latin terms for either 'Crusade' or 'Crusader' were widely used, and while there are several possible explanations for this, the most likely one is that the existing vocabulary for pilgrimage and pilgrims (*iter, peregrinatio, peregrini*) were considered adequate. In one of the most impressive early sculptural depictions of a Crusader, almost certainly representing Count Hugh I of Vaudémont, the Cross prominently displayed on the chest is accompanied by the traditional bag (scrip) and staff of the pilgrim. It is clear that the first Crusaders regarded themselves as pilgrims to Jerusalem; aside from the fact that they bore arms the chief thing which marked a departure from penitential practice to date was the unprecedented scope of the spiritual reward which they received.

The 'Anonymous' refers again and again to the Crusaders as *milites Christi*, soldiers or knights of Christ. It is a term which causes almost as much interpretative difficulty as the phrase 'Church of God' in the Clermont decree, but it forms a useful entry into the question of how crusading as holy war derived from eleventh-century society. It was a remarkable semantic hijack, because since patristic days the term had been applied to monks. Theirs was a spiritual combat against the devil, waged through prayer and worship, a combat for which their full withdrawal from the distractions and temptations of the world was essential. The military metaphor, which owed a lot to St Paul in Ephesians 6, was attractive to commentators in part because of the contrast with the plight of the soldier in the real world. So its application to actual soldiers was astonishing, a *volte face* in the Church's thinking which lies at the very heart of crusading. It is the more remarkable in so far as the word *milites* had acquired a more specific meaning by the late eleventh century: it was applied to Western Europe's fighting elite, men who wore chain mail and were trained to fight with spear and sword, usually on horse-back. Armsbearers in this sense had a very poor reputation in the eleventh century. In parts of France around 1000 they were regarded as a threat to social order, benefiting from the collapse of monarchical authority to impose the will of their lords on whole regions through brutality, arson and threats. By 1095 the connotations of being a knight (*miles*), and practising the skills of knighthood (*militia*) had become much less negative. Noblemen boasted of their possession of *militia* and *milites* as a group were consolidating into a distinctive stratum within the aristocracy, albeit with a heavy emphasis on their skills as warriors and a strong sense of deference toward their lords, a smaller group characterized by their possession of extensive lands, castles, well-established ancestry, and the extractive and juridical rights of lordship (*seigneurie*). But *milites* were still regarded as particularly prone to the sins of pride and greed: stone carvings showed them being dragged down to hell by demons on that account. The word *militia* was only one letter different from *malitia*, the Latin for evil, a coincidence that opened up many opportunities for word-play.

Moreover, the past misdeeds of the knightly class and their ancestors could not be ignored because they were enshrined in one of their principal sources of income, the 'customs' (*consuetudines*) through which they collected tribute in money or kind from villages which lacked effective protection, especially those owned by religious houses. Castellans in particular had often used their strongholds and garrisons to maintain a reign of terror over the surrounding 'district' (from the Latin *distringere* = to coerce). In the worst cases this was little more than formalized extortion, and some of the best examples can be found in charters in which knights who had taken the Cross agreed to renounce the custom in exchange for a one-off contribution towards their crusading expenses. A famous case is that of Nivelo of Chartres. The monks of the abbey of Saint Père de Chartres gave Nivelo ten pounds of silver in exchange for his agreement to:

> '...renounce forever in favour of St Peter an oppressive behaviour resulting from a certain bad custom, handed on to me not by ancient right but from the time of my father, a man of little weight who first harassed the poor with this oppression'.

The scribe spelled out the details with some relish.

> 'Whenever the onset of knightly ferocity stirred me up, I used to descend on Emprainville, taking with me a troop of my knights and a crowd of my attendants, and against nature I would make over the goods of the men of St Peter for food for my knights.'

The language employed here is melodramatic, expressing the horror of the monks at the illegality of the procedure, but there is much evidence that both for the monks and for the Crusaders there was a pleasing symmetry in the fact that the renunciation of these brutal practices was being incorporated into the Crusade. Financial and spiritual preparations converged: Crusaders were told that it was pointless to depart for Jerusalem without first clearing their consciences.

There was only one way for men like Nivelo to become 'knights of Christ', through a wholesale transformation of outlook achieved by the penitential process of taking up Christ's Cross. In the eyes of clerics this was a true conversion, and some accounts of the First Crusade contain conversion narratives as powerfully phrased as Bunyan's *Pilgrim's Progress*. One of these was Ralph of Caen's description of how Tancred, Bohemond of Taranto's nephew, responded to the news of the Crusade. 'Frequently he burned with anxiety because the warfare he engaged in as a knight seemed to be contrary to the Lord's commands', Ralph claimed. 'His mind was divided, uncertain whether to follow in the footsteps of the Gospel or the world.' Then came news of the Crusade and 'his vigour was aroused, his powers grew, his eyes opened, his courage was born'. The contrast between the old warfare and the new lent itself to effective rhetoric, and it made excellent sermon material because it focused the attention of listeners both on the extent and cause of their sinfulness and on its remedy. Version after version of Urban II's own sermon dwelt on the theme. But it achieved its classic formulation in Guibert of Nogent:

> 'God has instituted in our time holy wars, so that the order of knights and the crowd running in their wake… might find a new way of gaining salvation. And so they are not forced to abandon secular affairs completely by choosing the monastic life or any religious profession, as used to be the custom, but can attain in some measure God's grace while pursuing their own careers, with the liberty and in the dress to which they are accustomed.'

Naturally Guibert's view of the first Crusaders is tendentious. It represents the Crusade as a triumph of the Church in persuading knights to use their energy and skills for a good purpose while securing forgiveness for the sinfulness which was inherent in their way of life. All too easily the flow of influence can be reversed. The Crusade can then be seen as the culmination of a long process in which the rejection of violence which was integral to the teachings of the early Church was subverted by the ideology of a warrior aristocracy presiding over a thoroughly militarized society and constantly in search of land and booty. From this point of view the undoubted sophistication and learning of men like Guibert of Nogent, and for that matter Urban II, constituted mere camouflage. It is true that the eleventh century witnessed the cultural exaltation of virtues which were primarily associated with combat, either directly (physical strength and courage) or indirectly (loyalty). Not long after the First Crusade they received their apotheosis in the first great 'chanson de geste', *The Song of Roland*. It is often pointed out that Urban II was very much in tune with aristocratic values: he was the son of a Champagne castellan. Some of the themes which rapidly became prominent in Crusade preaching, such as the idea that Crusaders were 'vassals of Christ' called to perform a moral duty to defend the patrimonial lands of a great lord, were planted fairly and squarely in martial codes of honour. An argument can be constructed to the effect that some six centuries after the fall of Rome, the Church had finally lost the struggle to replace barbarian values with Christian ones.

3. Frankish and Muslim armies during the First Crusade.

But such an argument would be just as one-sided as the acceptance, at face value, of Guibert of Nogent's elevation of crusading to a secular equivalent of the monastic vocation. In the decades leading up to the council of Clermont the Church was certainly conscious of the problems posed by the endemic violence of the *milites*, especially in France. Urban II had been a monk of Cluny, the great religious house in Burgundy, and Cluny had built up a reputation for concern about how the lay aristocracy could achieve salvation. But churchmen in general were increasingly aware of the need to communicate the Christian message more effectively to people who were either unable or unwilling to follow the ideal path to salvation represented by the monastic life. It is true that the language, symbols and behaviour of some leading churchmen were influenced by military values. Urban II's predecessor, Gregory VII (1073–85), who was probably the first Pope to espouse penitential violence, had even dated two of his letters 'while on campaign' ('data in expeditione'). But at the heart of the papal programme of outreach to the laity was a cluster of ideas which were fundamentally religious in nature: the intimate relationship between Jerusalem and the Church's mission; the idea that one got closer to Christ through the exercise of charity (love), in the case of Crusaders love of God and of oppressed fellow-Christians in the East; and the encouragement of suitable penitential behaviour.

In practice there is no need to regard the First Crusade either as a clerical brainchild which was successfully 'sold' to a compliant laity, or as the creation of a bellicose and expansionist lay society thinly disguised as a religious exercise. For it is apparent that much of the thinking of the Crusaders, at least those of whom we know anything substantial, those of noble birth, derived from several generations of rich interaction between their families and a host of monastic houses. Increasingly Urban's call to Crusade in 1095 is seen not as a bolt from the blue but as an organic development in the protracted process by which noble families had entered religious houses and bestowed on them generous donations of land, rents and rights. It is not surprising that this regular but essentially humdrum pulse of activity has been neglected in favour of more spectacular events, the pronouncements of popes like Gregory VII and Urban II or 'proto-Crusades' like the campaigns of the early Spanish *Reconquista*. But it is in these links with religious houses, especially in the charters written to record major bequests, that we find many of the essential ways of thinking which would come to characterize Crusaders. In making their preparations for departure in 1095–6 moreover, many Crusaders turned for support to the same houses, so we get a close view (mediated, it is true, through the scribes) of the religious attitudes and motivations of those embarking on the expedition.

What we encounter in all of these charters is individuals whose piety had much in common with what the Church wanted to encourage, with subtle differences which showed that they were their own masters. They showed a more acute awareness of how particular aspects of their lives generated sin, greater concern about the degree of punishment which they would suffer on this account after death, and urgency in demanding to know how energetic action on their own parts would remedy matters. They had what churchmen regarded as a disturbingly literal view of intervention in the affairs of the world by God and the saints. Evidence was looked for, and if it failed to appear the result was not just disappointment but a loss of veneration. And while they respected monks, they did not revere them. They were not beyond criticizing them and making fun of their ways, and they engaged in lengthy and acrimonious litigation about lands which it was alleged that their own ancestors had granted away. What emerges from these charters is a nobility intensely anxious about its salvation, obsessed with honour, steering a bizarre course between generosity and parsimony, and possessing a strong sense of family solidarity and pride.

This last point is important because while the crusading message was directed at an individual's sense of sinfulness, that individual's response was conditioned by the attitude of the entire family. There was a market economy in Western Europe by 1095 and it is clear that frantic activity occurred in 1095–6 as land was sold or pledged to raise cash for the forthcoming Crusade. For this the charters issued by religious houses again constitute our best evidence: preparations for the Crusade received just a few words in the *GF* and not much more in other accounts of the Crusade. What the charters reveal is that families made considerable sacrifices to send their members to the East. More remarkably, some families were better disposed towards the Crusade than others were and they sent several members, which involved an even greater outlay although, of course, it also provided a useful support network. Any interpretation of the response to the Crusade which hinges on the expectation of material reward flounders in the face of this discovery. This applies especially to the once-popular idea that the Crusade was a kind of dumping ground for younger sons who could not expect to inherit any of the family's lands. If options were considered rationally, it would have been much easier and cheaper in 1095–6 to purchase a good estate for a younger son than to send him off on the Crusade, given the fall of land values which was caused by the universal demand for silver. This is not to say that deeply ingrained habits of acquisitiveness did not manifest themselves during the Crusade; but motivation cannot always be inferred from behaviour.

Thanks, above all, to the use of monastic charters we have a much fuller view of individual preparations for the First Crusade than we could once have dreamt of. The same does not apply to the process by which these Crusaders came together into the several armies, which collectively made up the Crusade. One thing we can say with certainty is that there were two waves, which set out at different times. The first wave was made up of forces led by Walter Sansavoir ('the penniless'), who was a knight from Poissy, and a preacher with enormous charisma called Peter the Hermit. They set out in the spring of 1096, just a few months after the council of Clermont and in advance of the departure date set by the Pope, which was 15 August. This was a mistake since it meant that they marched at a time of dearth, before the summer harvest of 1096 was in. After difficulties crossing the Balkans the two forces met up at Constantinople and crossed the Bosporus. But in a series of encounters with the Turks these Crusaders were defeated and more or less wiped out, though Peter the Hermit survived to play an important role at various points in the Crusade. This inglorious end was matched by a shameful beginning. In May and June 1096 members of the first wave led by Emich Count of Floheim, a highly unstable individual, attacked the Jewish communities at Speyer, Worms, Mainz and Cologne. Thousands were despoiled of their possessions and killed, including the entire community at Mainz, and the synagogues at Mainz and Cologne were burnt down. Jews were attacked too at Trier, Metz, and a number of smaller towns in the Rhine valley. Some Jews were forced to accept baptism, while others preferred to commit suicide: the chronicler Salomon bar Simson wrote that 'the women slaughtered their sons and daughters and then themselves'.

This first wave of Crusaders used to be considered as fundamentally different from what followed it. Sometimes called the 'People's Crusade', it was characterized as undisciplined, poorly organized and uncontrollable, features which brought about both the anti-Jewish pogroms in Germany and the catastrophic defeats in Anatolia. It is not a view found in the GF, which portrays Peter the Hermit as effectively commanding an advance guard. In recent years the idea that these armies failed because they contained few or no knights has been questioned. The corollary is that the massacres in the Rhineland were not aberrations but flowed naturally enough from crusading ideas. The gist was crystal clear: if Christ's enemies were to be attacked in the East because they were occupying his lands, why not start with the descendants of those who had actually nailed him to the Cross? This was a clear example, right at the start of the Crusade, of crusading attitudes forming in the grey area where clerical and lay values met. Assaults on Jews, including the use of coercion to bring about baptism, were something which the Church did not sanction, and there were attempts by clerics to shelter the Jews at Speyer, Worms and Mainz. But the Church did accept the idea of violence carried out in revenge, and for nobles in particular crusading as a form of vengeance was deeply attractive. It brought together their tendency towards violence and their empathy with Christ's suffering humanity. Baldric of Bourgueil makes this tendency all too clear in a sermon which he attributes to a Crusade-preacher:

'I address fathers and sons, brothers and nephews. If an outsider were to strike any of your kin down would you not avenge your blood relative? How much more ought you to avenge your God, your father, your brother, whom you see reproached, banished from his estates, crucified.'

This revision of views about the first wave of Crusaders has important consequences for the whole Crusade. There can be no doubt that the

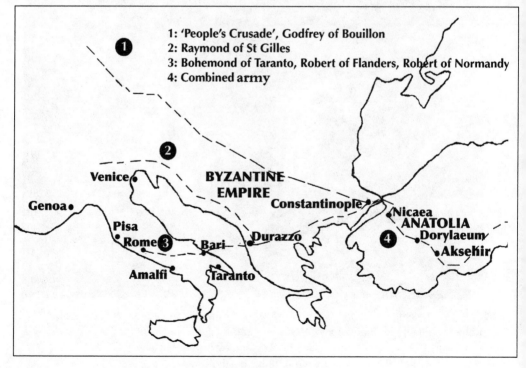

4. Map of the routes taken by the armies of the First Crusade.

5. The effigy of Robert Curthose, Duke of Normandy, at Gloucester Cathedral.
Robert, William the Conqueror's eldest son and one of the leaders of the First Crusade, was
imprisoned in England by his brother
Henry I until his death in 1134.

eastward march of the second wave, which departed in August 1096, was better managed than its predecessor's. The 'Anonymous' wrote, accurately enough, of three main groups. The first, led by Godfrey of Bouillon, marched to Constantinople by way of river valleys: the Danube, Morava and Maritza. The second, under Raymond of St Gilles, Count of Toulouse, crossed northern Italy and then chose the more difficult route southward through the Dalmatian mountains, before joining the old Roman *Via Egnatia* at Durazzo. The third army crossed the Adriatic at Bari and also followed the *Via Egnatia* from Durazzo to Constantinople; it included a group of great lords, Bohemond of Taranto, Robert, Count of Flanders, and Robert, Duke of Normandy, the eldest son of William the Conqueror. These groups were commanded by important men, described as 'princes' (*principes*) or 'big-shots' (*maiores*), they were expected to make decisions and their leadership was taken for granted not just by their household knights and feudal dependants but by most Crusaders who held lands in the regions which they governed. Their presence gave the second wave cohesion, structure and leadership. But all these features were much more rudimentary than would have been the norm for armies in the West. For each crusading group was accompanied by vast numbers of pilgrims, including women. And there was from the start a remarkable fluidity about the Crusade, with groups of varying size arriving and abandoning the venture all the time. In these circumstances the use of the word army, or its medieval equivalent 'host', becomes rather questionable. This bedevils the issue of numbers to such an extent that even rough quantification is extraordinarily difficult. When the groups of the second wave converged it is possible that they reached 50,000 in total; and one estimate for both waves has been put at 100,000. What is certain is that in the context of the time these were very large figures and that the scale as well as the nature of the First Crusade had no precedent in the centuries since the fall of Rome. It resembled a migration rather than a march, which helped create the impression that the Crusaders intended to settle in the East.

It is easy to imagine the reaction of the Byzantine Emperor, Alexius Comnenus, when these huge forces began to arrive outside Constantinople. Writing many years later, his daughter Anna captured well the mood of the moment:

> '...full of enthusiasm and ardour they thronged every highway, outnumbering the sand of the sea shore or the stars of heaven, carrying palms and bearing crosses on their shoulders. Like tributaries joining a river from all directions they streamed towards us in full force.'

6. Manuscript showing the siege of Antioch.

At no point did the Byzantine Greeks have any understanding of crusading, because all its constituent elements, with the exception of pilgrimage, were rooted in a society which had long since taken paths radically different from theirs. This makes their reaction highly interesting. Lacking any insight into the dynamics of the exercise, they fell back on intuition, and their intuitive response, or at least that of the most detailed contemporary source, Anna Comnena, seems very modern. 'The simpler folk', Anna wrote in her eulogistic life of her father, the *Alexiad*:

'...were led on by a desire to worship at our Lord's tomb and visit the holy places, but the more villainous characters had an ulterior purpose, for they hoped on their journey to seize the capital (Constantinople) itself.'

This was not an unreasonable supposition, given the fact that between 1081 and 1085 Bohemond had fought alongside his father, Robert Guiscard, in Balkan campaigning which had the seizure of Constantinople as its ultimate goal. Norman hostility towards the Byzantine Greeks is reflected throughout the *GF* in the abusive epithets ritually attached to Alexius's name, such as 'the wicked Emperor' or 'the miserable Emperor', which make him sound like a pantomime villain. To some extent this phraseology is the legacy of the way relations between Byzantines and Crusaders deteriorated as the march continued. But the more lurid passages of graecophobia were probably inserted into the *GF* when Bohemond took the text to France in 1106 to help arouse enthusiasm for a new Crusade; he anticipated that it would have to fight not just the Muslims but the Byzantines and he wanted to present the latter in as bad a light as possible.

Protecting Constantinople from a surprise attack was Alexius's primary goal; thus the Crusaders were only allowed into the city in very small groups. But he was also aware of the opportunity that the Crusade presented to regain some of the territory which had been Byzantine before the Seljuq Turks had overrun it in the 1070s and 1080s. This meant all the land stretching from Nicaea, which was in northern Anatolia, not far from Constantinople, as far as Antioch in northern Syria. It had constituted some of the most valuable provinces in the empire. If Alexius could regain this land, then his original approach to Urban II in 1095, which had triggered the Clermont sermon, would prove remarkably fruitful, despite the fact that the forces which had appeared could scarcely be more different from the bands of mercenary knights that he had had in mind, serving for pay and leaving once they had it. The Emperor made a good start, cleverly establishing a form of control over the Crusade's leaders by using the feudal links with which they were familiar. All the great lords except Raymond of St Gilles swore allegiance to him as his vassals; and even Raymond swore a modified form of oath to Alexius. Byzantine-Crusader co-operation was sealed by the capture of Nicaea in June 1097, which was the Crusade's first success.

The *GF* is so permeated with its author's anti-Greek sentiments that it loses credibility on the early phase of the expedition, but as the Crusaders marched south-eastward across Anatolia the author's unadorned style and constant touches of telling detail come into their own. There is no need to question the accuracy with which the 'Anonymous' described the Crusaders' first major victory in battle against the Turks, at Dorylaeum on 1 July 1097, or the sufferings which they went through, first while traversing the Anatolian plateau and then in crossing the anti-Taurus mountain range to reach Antioch. Arriving at Antioch in October 1097, the Crusaders entered the most difficult phase of their venture. They did not proceed southward to Jerusalem until early in 1099. What detained them was a combination of Turkish resistance and internal disunity. Antioch was far too significant simply to be passed by. The 'Anonymous' paid it the compliment of pausing in his narrative in order to describe its strength and distinction. It was an extremely well-fortified city defended by about 5,000 men, and a good deal of it, including its citadel, had been built on the steep slopes of Mount Silpius. It was not until March 1098 that the Crusaders succeeded even in mounting an effective blockade, and the capture of the city on 3 June 1098 was only achieved through the treachery of an officer in the Turkish garrison called Firuz. Even then the citadel, 'a wonderful building which is exceedingly strong', remained in Turkish hands.

At Antioch, moreover, the Crusaders came to the attention of the major Turkish power-brokers in Syria, Ridwan of Aleppo, Duqaq of Damascus and Kerbogha of Mosul. It is often pointed out that the single most important factor in helping the First Crusade succeed was the deaths in 1092 not just of the Seljuq Sultan Malikshah, but also of the vizier, Nizam al-Mulk, the power behind the throne for thirty years. The heartland of the Seljuq sultanate in Iran turned into a battleground for the rival sons of Malik Shah. Meanwhile Seljuq power in Syria and Palestine fragmented. It is true that a pitched battle against a united Seljuq army would probably have proved disastrous for the Crusaders. Encounters with separate relief armies dispatched from Damascus and Mosul were difficult enough. But the defeat of

7. Coins of Bohemond I, Prince of Antioch.

Kerbogha's army on 28 June 1098, promptly followed by the surrender of the citadel in Antioch, finally opened up the road to Jerusalem.

The Crusaders agreed to begin the march on 1 November but when that day came a major dispute flared up over the long-term possession of Antioch. The pro-Byzantine lobby amongst the Crusaders, led by Raymond of St Gilles, wanted to hand the city back to Alexius Comnenus, even though Byzantine assistance to the Crusade had become fitful at best. Bohemond staked a personal claim to the city largely on the basis of his having bribed Firuz and thereby gained Antioch for the Crusaders. This was more than bickering over booty. The future shape of a Frankish establishment in the Holy Land was implicitly being debated, with two alternatives on offer: one of Frankish holdings in Palestine being protected by, and effectively subject to, a restored Byzantine empire in Syria; the other of a triumphalist Frankish presence stretching from Antioch southward, enjoying an uneasy and even a competitive relationship with Constantinople. One of the most fateful events in the Crusade occurred in late June 1098, when Alexius Comnenus was at Aksehir (Philomelium) in Anatolia, leading an army to assist the Crusaders. A group of deserters, including Stephen of Blois, William the Conqueror's son-in-law, encountered the Emperor and justified their own flight by assuring him that Kerbogha's army would have wiped out the Crusaders by the time he could reach them. Faced with the danger of being cut off from Constantinople, Alexius reluctantly turned back.

The impasse over Antioch came to hinge on Raymond of St Gilles, a complex man whose actions are hard to interpret. His chaplain, Raymond of Aguilers, wrote a first-hand narrative of the Crusade but it does not eulogize Raymond, in the way that the *GF* does Bohemond or the *Alexiad* Alexius Comnenus. Raymond of Aguilers was more interested in visions than decision-making, and he was more violently hostile to the Greeks than the 'Anonymous' – he had no time for his lord's defence of the interests of Alexius Comnenus and this distorted his account. What seems to have happened is that by Christmas 1098 Raymond of St Gilles was being pulled in two directions: he had no desire to give in to Bohemond over Antioch, but he felt a particular sympathy for the poor Crusaders, who suffered terrible famine in the winter months because the army had been stationary for so long. In January 1099 a sort of popular demonstration took place, in which the fortifications of Raymond's base at Ma'arrat-an-Numan were pulled down. This precipitated Raymond's decision to continue southward, and one-by-one the other leaders joined him, with the exception of Bohemond. The advance on Jerusalem proved to be relatively straightforward. A series of Turkish and Arab lords hastened to make deals, which enabled the Crusaders to avoid further sieges while replenishing their horses and supplies. The one siege they did undertake, at 'Arqah in the Lebanon, they abandoned in May in favour of a dash to take Jerusalem while food supplies remained buoyant.

On 7 June 1099 the Crusaders arrived at Jerusalem. There was an urgency in their approach towards this siege. In 1098 the Fatimid rulers of Egypt had taken advantage of the disruption caused by the arrival of the Crusade to retake Jerusalem from the Seljuq Turks, and a large army led by the vizier, al-Afdal, was soon on its way to relieve the city. After a month little progress had been made and it was clear that a large-scale effort would have to be invested in building siege machines. With timber transported by camel from as far away as Samaria, and nails and rope brought from Christian vessels which had docked at Jaffa, ladders and two siege towers were constructed. The final assault started in the night of 13–14 July. There were two attacks, the first directed by Raymond of St Gilles on a section of wall in the south-west, and the second by Godfrey of Bouillon in the north-east. After more than a day of hard fighting, it was Godfrey's men who breached the walls. The first across were two Flemish knights, Gilbert and Litold of Tournai. The massacres then began. As Bill Clinton pointed out in his 2001 Dimbleby lecture, it was not only Muslims who fell: the Jews of Jerusalem, who sought refuge in their synagogue, were also slaughtered. The worst massacre of

Muslims occurred on the Temple Mount. Here Tancred offered his protection to many Muslims who had taken refuge in the al-Aqsa mosque, but other Crusaders managed to break in and killed them too. Very shortly after the capture of Jerusalem Godfrey of Bouillon defeated Raymond of St Gilles in the election to be its first ruler, assuming the title: 'Advocate of the Holy Sepulchre' because he declined to be king in the city in which Christ had worn the crown of thorns. Jerusalem had been seized and its future government settled, but as the 'Anonymous' realized, the true end of the First Crusade was the encounter with al-Afdal's army. This took place near Ascalon, south-west of Jerusalem, on 11 August, and resulted in a resounding victory for the Crusaders. 'Our men came back to Jerusalem rejoicing': although still highly precarious, the Frankish hold over Jerusalem was at least secure from any immediate threat. In September those great lords who had not won lands for themselves in the East, Raymond of St Gilles, Robert of Flanders and Robert of Normandy, began the long journey home.

The hopes and ambitions of leaders like Bohemond of Taranto, Raymond of St Gilles and Godfrey of Bouillon are endlessly interesting, and none are straightforward. It might seem, for example, that Bohemond's career before, during and after the Crusade bears out Anna Comnena's distinction between those who were driven by piety and those who wanted to gain land – his antagonism towards Byzantium and his single-minded defence of his claim to Antioch fit the stereotype of the ambitious and ruthless Norman *conquistador*. Anna portrayed him as thoroughly duplicitous ('by nature a liar') but charming, energetic and resourceful. Yet the Normans were famous for their piety and it is anachronistic to portray Bohemond coldly pursuing a policy of conquest camouflaged with piety. As for the rivalry between Raymond and Godfrey over Jerusalem, this remains as shrouded in mystery as many papal elections of the period. We have good grounds for believing that Raymond actively sought the post, but the origins of Godfrey's candidacy are as unclear as the nature of the college that elected him. In fact the election of 1099 was the suitable culmination of a Crusade whose management had throughout been characterized by *ad hoc* and erratic formulations for making decisions. The natural leader for the Crusade was Alexius Comnenus and when he declined to accompany the Crusaders southward in the spring of 1097 the great lords could find no alternative commander.

Ineffective leadership therefore featured among the many problems facing the first Crusaders. On most of these thousands of individuals we have no information at all, but for the expedition as a whole we possess an unusually large amount of evidence. This enables us to build up a convincing composite picture, one which complements what I have already said on the origins of crusading. It is important first to reiterate how much suffering the Crusaders endured, because it was so much a part of the experience. Those who were present from first to last served three years in the field. They were fighting against an enemy whose military techniques were new to them, and in an unfamiliar and hostile climate and terrain. Their horses died under them and their tents rotted around them. Their sense of isolation was acute – in their letters home Crusaders constantly begged their families and communities to pray for them. Fear, disease and high levels of stress are constantly present in the sources. During the crossing of the anti-Taurus range, with chargers and pack animals alike plummeting from precipices, the 'Anonymous' described knights paralyzed with anxiety:

> '...wringing their hands because they were so frightened and miserable, not knowing what to do with themselves and their armour, and offering to sell their shields, valuable breastplates and helmets for 3d or 5d or any price they could get'.

Worn down by the march, the Crusaders were ill-equipped to face the successive periods of famine, which they encountered. The first took place during the first phase of the siege of Antioch, in the winter of 1097–8. A stationary army of up to 50,000 quickly ran through not just its own supplies but anything which the surrounding countryside could provide. Prices soared and the 'Anonymous' narrated laconically that 'many of our people died there, not having the means to buy at so dear a rate'. The activities of the Turks made the situation worse. A grim war of attrition developed. The garrison, ably commanded by Yaghisiyan, constantly carried out daring raids against the Crusaders, and their allies outside the city inflicted such heavy losses on foraging parties that the knights started refusing to perform escort duty. This was a very grim development given the emphasis which such men placed on their honour and reputation. Then came the capture of Antioch and the arrival of Kerbogha's army, which kept the Crusaders bottled up within the city. Inflation again set in and some resorted to eating ground vegetation. 'We endured this misery, hunger and fear for twenty-six days.' Given these circumstances it is astonishing that a solemn three-day fast was decreed before the Crusaders joined battle with Kerbogha in June 1098. Yet worse was to come. A third famine set in during the winter of 1098–9 as the army failed to move southward. Some Crusaders were driven to dig up the corpses of their recently interred enemies and cook them.

Naturally these traumatic events did not affect all the Crusaders alike. Knights were more effectively supplied in the first place and better placed to forage as well as to afford famine prices. On the other hand they seem to have been more easily demoralized, upset by the deaths of their chargers, by military reverses and slow progress. There were some highly emotional scenes, such as when William, Lord of Melun, was bitterly reproached by Bohemond for trying to desert (together with Peter the Hermit) during the second period of famine; before he received his dressing down William 'spent the whole of the night in my lord Bohemond's tent, lying on the ground like so much rubbish'. Knights who became impoverished, wounded or diseased, and lacked the support of kinsmen, descended into the ranks of the poor. These grew as the Crusade progressed, though there were always large numbers of them. All the leaders accepted a responsibility for keeping them alive but it seems to have been Raymond of St Gilles who felt it most strongly. In February or March 1099 it seems that Raymond gave Peter the Hermit a quasi-official post as 'guardian' of the interests of the poor. The papal legate on the Crusade, Adhémar Bishop of Le Puy, also did his best to look after them and even preached a form of social contract, telling the knights that 'none of you can be saved if he does not respect the poor and succour them; you cannot be saved without them, and they cannot survive without you'.

It is tempting to take one's cue from Adhémar and divide the Crusade into three main groups: the knights, the poor and the clerics. This has the advantage of fitting an idea much in vogue at the time of the Crusade that society at large was divided into three 'orders', people who fought (*bellatores*), laboured (*laboratores*) and prayed (*oratores*). It was expressed by one of the Crusaders, Anselm of Ribemont, in a letter home in which he asked Archbishop Manasses of Reims to:

> '...provide for our land, so that both the nobles live in concord among themselves, and the people labour in security on that which is theirs, and the ministers of Christ be free to devote themselves to the Lord'.

In reality, though, the triadic schema fitted neither contemporary society nor the Crusade that well. There was considerable social mobility, upward as well as downward: the impoverished knight had his counterpart in the knight who enjoyed a windfall of booty, took others into his service, and was able to play the lord. Nor was there any division between combatants and civilians, any able-bodied male pilgrim who could use a weapon was expected to fight. Raymond of Aguilers's figures for combatants in the assault on Jerusalem were 12,000 arms-bearers including between 1,200 and 1,300 knights, a ratio of 9:1. At Jerusalem every member of the army who was not sick, including the knights, joined in the common task of constructing siege engines, despite the conditions of appalling thirst in which they laboured. Most importantly, the three-order approach does not account for two important groups of Crusaders who call for separate treatment: sailors and women.

The fact that none of the contingents on the Crusade went East by sea has tended to disguise the important role which sea power played in securing victory. At various points in the Crusade the army received assistance from ships coming from Genoa, Pisa, Venice, Constantinople and England. Their contribution was varied. During the first period of serious famine at Antioch, around Christmas 1097, it is quite possible that the supplies which they brought across from Cyprus staved off mass starvation. The timber, tools, nails and rope which these vessels carried proved invaluable at the sieges of Antioch and Jerusalem, as did the skills of their crews both in construction and in combat. There is much that is mysterious about some of these naval contingents, not least the origins and identity of the 'English', who were most likely Anglo-Saxons in Byzantine service. But some of them certainly had taken the Cross. In the Italian maritime communes there was a lively appreciation of the potential which the Crusade opened up for forging stronger trading links with the Levant, but it was accompanied by a surge of religious enthusiasm. Trade and Crusade were perfectly compatible.

The part played by female Crusaders is even more difficult to quarry from the sources than the role of sea power is. Urban II had attempted to exclude women but the dominant profile of the expedition, as a penitential pilgrimage, rendered this futile. Women accompanied the army as individual pilgrims, wives, servants and camp followers. At the battle of Dorylaeum (1 July 1097) they were a source of practical assistance to the combatants, earning the praise of the 'Anonymous':

> 'The women in our camp were a great help to us that day, for they brought up water for the fighting men to drink, and gallantly encouraged those who were fighting and defending them.'

But the circumstances at Dorylaeum were exceptional. In their march from Nicaea the Crusaders had divided for the sake of convenience into two columns. Those in the first column, which included the Normans, were all but surrounded by the Turks and beat off their attacks for five or six hours before being relieved by the arrival of the second column. So the fighting took place on the very fringes of an embattled camp, it was tough and it lasted an unusually long time. Such a chance for the women to assist did not recur, and when the 'Anonymous' mentions them during the remainder of the Crusade in relation to military actions, it is usually as incidental casualties, such as the unnamed woman in Bohemond's camp who was killed by an arrow during the siege of Antioch. Aside from this they feature largely in a sexual capacity, as sources of sin. This was especially true of the accounts of the Crusade which were written by Raymond of Aguilers, Fulcher of Chartres and the north French cluster of Benedictine monks, who were misogynists by training. There are many signs that women were deeply attracted by the crusading message, but they were thrust into a marginal position in military terms, and viewed as a spiritual threat to the Crusade's chances of success.

Whichever group they belonged to, the Crusaders handled their gruelling experience in two ways: on the one hand they fell back on familiar ways and responses and on the other they adapted and improvised. Eleventh-century society derived massive coherence from the proliferation of ties of dependency and lordship. These were carried onto the Crusade and accentuated by the need of so many dependants for on-going support in the essentials of life. But some lords lost their ability to meet these obligations, so ties of lordship fell into a state of flux. This was most dramatic in the case of knights: some Crusaders whose families had been feudal dependants of others for generations, holding valuable lands from them as fiefs, maybe even coming on Crusade as an expression of their feudal loyalty, were compelled to transfer that loyalty to another lord during the course of the Crusade. All parties to such arrangements knew that they were temporary and that normal relations would resume once they were back in the West. The 'Anonymous' himself left the service of Bohemond during the last phase of the Crusade, probably joining the group recruited by a knight called Raymond Pilet, who was himself a dependant of Raymond of St Gilles. In some ways therefore the Crusade saw a reassertion of the personal aspect of feudal ties, running against the trend, which had now become dominant in the West, to stabilize those ties by anchoring them in land tenure.

Yet land also played its part on the Crusade. One remarkable feature of the long period of immobility at Antioch was that all of the great lords established bases in northern Syria, where they maintained caches of food and arms and controlled the villages of the surrounding countryside. These became their 'lands' (*terrae*) and they formed a rough circle around Antioch.

After the defeat of Kerbogha in June 1098, when it was decided to disperse until November:

> '...our leaders separated and each went off into his own territory ('in terram suam') until it should be time to resume the march. They had it announced throughout the city that if there were any poor man, lacking gold and silver, who wished to take service with them and stay on, they would gladly enrol him'.

The exercising of power through the possession of land and fortified places was so deeply ingrained in the *modus operandi* of these men that they automatically resorted to it even in this thoroughly alien environment. But as the passage shows, it was also a means of keeping the army together – habit and the dictates of survival formed a rough and ready alliance.

This last point is vital for understanding the Crusaders' approach towards booty. One of the passages in the *GF* that has provoked most comment is the message which was passed along the line at the battle of Dorylaeum, 'Stand fast all together, trusting in Christ and in the victory of the Holy Cross. Today, please God, you will all gain much booty'. This jaunty juxtaposition of faith and profit has been seized on with glee by commentators who are convinced that the Crusaders were interested mainly in material profit. But the issue was not so straightforward. An inflow of booty was essential to oil the wheels of lordship and, more basically, to feed the army, either directly or through barter and exchange. The booty taken at Dorylaeum itself included 'gold, silver, horses, asses, camels, oxen and sheep', a mixture of precious metals, pack animals and meat, all no doubt replacing items originally assembled at the start of the Crusade a year previously and by this point either traded, lost or consumed. The same holds true of the Crusaders' other victories. After their defeat of Kerbogha at Antioch:

> '...the enemy left his pavilions, with gold and silver and many furnishings, as well as sheep, oxen, horses, mules, camels and asses, corn, wine, flour and many other things of which we were badly in need'.

And after the battle of Ascalon:

> '...our men went back to the enemy camp and found innumerable spoils of gold and silver, piles of riches, and all kinds of

animals, weapons and tools. They took what they wanted and burnt the rest'.

Booty was thus an indispensable fuel, consumed in vast quantities by the Crusade like a modern passenger jet-plane. Yet this does not wholly explain the obsession which the Crusaders had with material gain. The Crusade derived from a deeply acquisitive aristocratic society and it naturally reflected this acquisitiveness. There were good reasons for the care with which the Clermont Crusade decree specified that prospective Crusaders should be motivated by devotion rather than the prospect of gain. Like all churchmen, Urban II well knew that devotion rubbed shoulders with greed in the psychology of his audience. In their eyes it was dishonourable to be poor (unless one was a monk, a pauper by vocation) and incongruous to emerge from victory without gain. It was also commendable to take opportunities when they arose. One of the strangest passages in the *GF* is a conversation between Kerbogha of Mosul and his mother. She warns her son not to fight the Crusaders because their God is all-powerful and she read signs of his impending defeat in the stars. Kerbogha ignores her so she returns to Aleppo 'taking with her everything on which she could lay her hands'. This is not intended to be derogatory, rather it is seen as natural human behaviour, a projection onto the Muslims of Frankish values. Godfrey of Bouillon's younger brother, Baldwin of Boulogne, provided the most dramatic example of such opportunism. Early in 1098 Baldwin led a splinter group to Edessa, north-east of Antioch in the middle Euphrates, and set up a principality there. Frankish rule at Edessa was isolated and precarious. Though it proved a useful marcher-principality for Antioch, its seizure contributed little towards gaining or holding Jerusalem. Yet Baldwin seems to have escaped any criticism for his move and smoothly succeeded his brother Godfrey as ruler of Jerusalem in 1100. His chaplain Fulcher of Chartres noted, apparently without irony, that he grieved a little for the death of his brother but rejoiced more over his inheritance. Baldwin's equivalent amongst the Norman contingent, Bohemond's nephew Tancred, went as far as to place his standard over the church of the Nativity when he occupied Bethlehem: this was considered too much and he was heavily criticized for it.

Devotion and gain in fact were complementary – like a good lord, God rewarded those who waged his war. Repeatedly in their letters home, the Crusaders boasted of the spoils which they had won in God's service. In a letter to his wife in March 1098, Stephen of Blois rejoiced that he was twice as rich as he was when he set out. Recounting the events which took place at the capture of Jerusalem, the 'Anonymous' wrote two consecutive sentences in which he first described the looting of the city: 'the houses full of all sorts of goods', then narrated the influx of the Crusaders to the church of the Holy Sepulchre: 'rejoicing and weeping from excess of gladness'. There were dangers of course. One, the fear clearly expressed in the Clermont decree, was that greed would become the motivation of those who fought. A second, more practical, was that the desire for gain would hinder the efficiency of the Crusade as a military operation. But though this came close to wrecking the Crusade during the long dispute over the possession of Antioch, it does not seem to have been a serious problem at the level of the knights. Perhaps because they recognized the extremely dangerous situation which they faced in pitched battle, the Crusaders' discipline was remarkable. The destruction of the first wave of Crusaders in Anatolia may well have had a salutary effect on those who followed them.

In fact it was in the battles which they fought that the Crusaders showed themselves at their most adaptable. Nothing better disproves the stereotype of the blundering, block-headed, mail-clad knight than the extraordinarily clever way in which the Crusaders developed means of dealing with the threat posed by Turkish tactics. The Turks were expert archers who were skilled in firing while on horseback. In the ninth century an Arab writer graphically described that skill: 'The Turk can shoot at beasts, birds, hoops, men, sitting quarry, dummies and birds on the wing, and do so at full gallop to fore or to rear, to left or to right, upwards or downwards.' They used their speed and versatility in the saddle to confuse their opponents while inflicting casualties at a safe distance, 'skirmishing, throwing darts and javelins and shooting arrows from an astonishing range', as the 'Anonymous' put it. Their effective range was about sixty metres, so it was no wonder the Crusade's first wave was so easily cut to pieces. By contrast, the chief tactic of the Crusaders was the cavalry charge with couched lance, a weapon which only achieved its effect when launched against a compact, preferably stationary body of enemy troops. The Crusaders were undoubtedly lucky. They were thoroughly briefed on Turkish tactics by Alexius Comnenus and at their first major engagement, Dorylaeum, they had the advantage of surprise; this gave them the victory and enabled them to confirm Alexius's briefing by observing enemy tactics at close quarters. Thereafter, almost certainly at Bohemond's initiative, they took steps to prevent the Turks dispersing, and used the configurations of the landscape to their advantage. Most importantly, at the battle of Antioch the Crusaders were successful in concentrating Kerbogha's forces between the River Orontes and the hilly ground to the north-west of the city. In recent years it has been stressed that the demands made on the Crusaders to adapt were even greater because they lost so many mounts. By the time they fought Kerbogha they were probably reduced to only 200 chargers. The battle of Ascalon was different: the Fatimids used more conventional tactics than the Seljuq Turks, the Crusaders had replenished their chargers, and the shock charge had a devastating effect on the enemy. Overall, in circumstances where a single defeat could have proved disastrous, the Crusaders performed exceptionally well.

It is arguable that greed and indiscipline posed less of a threat to the Crusade than excessive religiosity. Fasting for several days before major engagements was bad enough; but on 8 July 1099 the entire crusading army processed barefoot around Jerusalem to beseech God's aid for the forthcoming assault on the city, an action which could have been very dangerous if the city's garrison had chosen to exploit it. The devotional aspect of the Crusade had many such extraordinary features and they were manifested from the start. One group of Crusaders who probably perished in the first wave followed a goose which they believed to be suffused with the Holy Spirit, and some Crusaders branded or tattooed crosses on their bodies. The Benedictine chroniclers of the early twelfth century drew an overall picture of the Crusade which resembled a Victorian sepia print, so pure in thought and action that it was, to quote one historian, 'a monastery in motion'. The catastrophic failure of a follow-up Crusade in 1101 actually assisted this idealization of the first Crusaders, who were seen to have possessed all the virtues (including great eloquence) while their successors wallowed in all the vices. The reality was of course different. Extremities of enthusiasm have always lent themselves to deception, and the First Crusade was no exception. One Crusader who had branded himself with the Cross raised funds to go to the East by claiming that the branding was the work of an angel. There were charlatans, cowards, deserters and apostates. And there were many camp followers. Guibert of Nogent, whose horror of sex was so extreme that he would have been a gift to Freud, shook his head over the Crusaders' adventures in Constantinople's state-run brothels. He wrote of unmarried women who became pregnant and were punished savagely, together with their pimps. When the clergy blamed military reverses on sexual behaviour, the Crusaders responded by expelling not just prostitutes but their own wives from the camp, though they did set up another camp for them nearby. Yet the fact remains that the First Crusade was, amongst other things, a remarkable example of collective devotion. Prominent aspects of religious practice were brought to the foreground thanks to the fear, uncertainties and stress which the Crusaders had constantly to confront.

At the core of the Crusaders' devotion was their own relationship with God. Every event in the Crusade was interpreted within this framework. It is hard for us today to push from our minds the fact that this was the first of many Crusades, to place ourselves in the shoes of men and women who were many hundreds of miles from home, conscious that failure could very easily cause them to share the fate of the Crusade's disastrous first wave and then to be ignominiously forgotten. Their battle cry, 'deus vult', had to be proved to be no less than the truth. In the *GF* this led to the repeated use of formulae restating the nature of the Crusade as a war mandated by God. Of this the Cross as well as the battle cry itself were constant reminders. So when Robert of Flanders engaged the enemy he was 'armed at all points with faith and with the sign of the Cross, which he bore loyally every day'. Bohemond was 'protected on all sides by the sign of the Cross', while the Crusaders generally were 'knights of the true God, armed at all points with the sign of the Cross'. Crusaders who perished during the expedition were regarded by their comrades as martyrs. This started with those who fell in the first wave, who 'were the first to endure blessed martyrdom for the name of our lord Jesus Christ'. Significantly, martyrdom was the reward not just of those Crusaders who died in action but also of those who starved to death. When the 'Anonymous' depicted both Kerbogha and al-Afdal commenting on the inferior quality of the Crusaders' weaponry, he was emphasizing the point that it was God, not the Crusaders themselves, who won the battles against them. At times God's participation was dramatic, taking the form of the dispatch of fighting saints to take part in actions, as at the battle of Antioch, where 'a countless host of men on white horses' assisted the Crusaders, commanded by Saints George, Mercurius and Demetrius. St George's intervention seems to have made the most impact, for it was represented in a number of paintings and sculptures in the West.

God did not supply his warriors with a blank cheque. The Crusade forfeited its worth as a penitential exercise when the Crusaders sinned. God's favour was then withdrawn, his punishment taking the form of military setbacks. These could be severe, though in a war which participants believed had been brought into being by God it was expected that they would stop short of annihilation – even God could go too far, and the 'Anonymous' portrays Bohemond's half-brother, who was in Byzantine service, threatening to abandon the faith altogether if rumours of the Crusade's destruction proved to be true. For most of the time the Crusade's penitential nature is hidden from sight because it was expressed in liturgical forms which, reassuring though they were to the Crusaders, were too unremarkable to need recording; but when failure occurred it becomes more conspicuous. The same applied to the spiritual preparations which were undertaken before major engagements. Fasting before battle, alms-giving to the poor, and the barefoot procession around the walls of Jerusalem, such were highlights in a quotidian round of penitential activity. During the engagements themselves the Crusaders did not lose sight of the need for God's support; at the siege of Ma'arrat-an-Numan the clerics formed a 'spiritual militia' (*militia spiritualis*), clustered behind the siege tower: 'clad in their holy vestments, praying and beseeching God to defend his people, and to exalt Christendom and cast down idolatry'.

Victory and defeat were at best crude indicators of the Crusaders' standing in God's eyes, nor did they communicate in any detail what the heavenly court wanted done; and with leadership undecided and much serious conflict over strategic issues, there was a massive need for such guidance. Attempts were made to meet it through visions. This was not in the least surprising. In eleventh-century religion death was far from being an insuperable chasm, and both the saints and dead kinsmen appeared to the living, warning, encouraging and giving instructions which were sometimes very precise. One role of relics was to act as portals through which saints could make such appearances. Members of a stressed and frequently starving army living in an atmosphere of highly charged religious enthusiasm were very prone to such visions, and though visions occurred during the preaching of the Crusade and in its early stages, there was an upsurge of visionary activity during the long period spent around Antioch. The 'Anonymous' gives details of the two most famous visionaries, a priest called Stephen of Valence and a peasant called Peter Bartholomew. Stephen was lying prostrate in the church of St Mary in Antioch in June 1098 when he experienced a vision featuring Christ, the Virgin and St Peter. It was very revealing: Christ assured Stephen that he would support the Crusade to the end but he expressed his dissatisfaction with the sexual immorality of the Crusaders; Mary and Peter fell at Christ's feet, 'praying and beseeching him to help his people in this tribulation'. This was a classic depiction of intercession at work. Christ relented and promised a sign of his assistance in five days time.

Stephen's vision was admonitory and consolatory – it carried no political message though Adhémar of Le Puy made adroit use of it to prise from the great lords an oath that they would not abandon the Crusade. Peter Bartholomew's visions were more momentous and carried more implications. In June 1098 he told Raymond of St Gilles that before Antioch fell he had had a series of visions in which St Andrew told him that the lance used to pierce Christ's side on the Cross was buried in the cathedral of St Peter in Antioch; the apostle had even magically transported the disbelieving Peter to the church and shown him exactly where the lance was buried. Now that Antioch was in Christian hands, it was possible to dig for the lance, and it was excavated in the very place indicated by Peter. According to the 'Anonymous', the discovery brought about an instantaneous lift in morale in an army which until then had been paralyzed by despondency: 'From that hour we decided on a plan of attack', and the leaders even dispatched an embassy to Kerbogha with extravagant terms, clearly expecting them to be scornfully rejected. Actually a fortnight passed before the Crusaders marched out to fight Kerbogha but the point was made.

Probably no other episode in the First Crusade provokes modern incredulity more emphatically than the discovery of the holy lance. Muslim chroniclers at the time saw it as a classic example of Christian gullibility. This scepticism is quite understandable. It would not have been difficult for Peter Bartholomew to conceal the lance before seeking out Raymond of St Gilles, especially if we follow some historians in interpreting the relic as the lance's head rather than as a full-length Roman spear. Some contemporaries formed the opinion that Peter was a charlatan. After the battle of Antioch he continued to have visions of St Andrew in which the saint's instructions were detailed and highly political. They were not politically charged in the way we might expect. For while Peter's visions favoured Raymond's leadership of the Crusade, they also advocated an immediate march southward, leaving Antioch in Bohemond's hands. Nonetheless, Peter was increasingly seen as partisan, and matters came to a head when he irritably responded to scepticism by demanding the right to undergo an ordeal by fire. The ordeal took place on Good Friday 1099 and he was so badly burned that he later died of his wounds. From this point onward veneration of the lance was confined largely to the Provençals, which may explain why the ordeal receives no treatment at all in the GF, since the 'Anonymous' was serving with them by this point.

If Peter Bartholomew was indeed a trickster, he handled his role with some skill, for his visions convincingly fitted a general pattern. During the last stage of the Crusade, from January 1099 onward, visions continued to be frequent despite the effective resolution of the dispute over Antioch. They were complemented by sightings of dead Crusaders returning as ghosts, such as Adhémar of le Puy scaling the walls of Jerusalem, while increasing numbers of relics were discovered. The culmination of this last process was the discovery of a relic of the True Cross near the church of the Holy Sepulchre in August 1099; such a find was a worthy substitute for the somewhat tarnished holy lance and it was treated with enormous veneration until lost in battle nearly a century later. Religious expectations rose steadily as the Crusaders came closer to Jerusalem itself, passing through the very towns and villages where Christ and the apostles had lived. Throughout the Crusade there had been a strong consciousness that the Crusaders were liberating the road to the Holy Sepulchre as well as themselves following it. The *GF* constantly reveals that Christ's Tomb was never far from their minds. While still in Anatolia the leaders agreed to a proposal by a knight called Peter d'Aups that he should hold a captured town 'in fealty to God and the Holy Sepulchre, our leaders and the Emperor'. Fighting at Antioch the Crusaders 'called on the name of Christ and put our trust in the pilgrimage to the Holy Sepulchre', and the Turks were defeated 'by the power of God and the Holy Sepulchre'. When Jerusalem was reached this association of pilgrimage and warfare was made crystal clear when the 'Anonymous' commented that 'our leaders decided to attack the city with engines, so that we might enter it and worship at our Saviour's Sepulchre'. Simply to bring the pilgrimage to a close, Jerusalem had to be captured.

The increasing excitement experienced during the march south was matched by a burgeoning triumphalism. The First Crusade need not have damaged relations between the various Christian Churches. One of the factors which brought it about was a rapprochement between the two principal ones, the Catholic and Orthodox, which encouraged Alexius Comnenus to approach the Pope for assistance. Sympathy for the oppressed Christians in the East featured strongly in the Pope's sermon at Clermont. But a number of circumstances converged to erode this ecumenism and replace it with a supremacist outlook. In the first place, it has been shown that from the start the goal of freeing the Eastern Christians lacked prominence in the thinking of the Crusaders. Their charters and letters reveal that their view of what they were about was solidly focused on the reoccupation of Jerusalem and the liberation of Christ's tomb. As papal legate, Bishop Adhémar of Le Puy was eloquent in expounding Urban II's rather broader views and wishes: for example, he ensured that the Greek patriarch of Antioch, expelled by the Turks, was reinstated when the city fell. But Adhémar died on 1 August 1098, just at the time when the ecumenist cause began to need his intervention most. Shortly after his death the Crusade's leaders wrote to the Pope asking him to come to the East in person and complete the Crusade with them. Antioch had been St Peter's first Episcopal seat and nothing could be more appropriate than the Pope entering it in triumph. The letter even referred to the Eastern Christians, 'Greeks and Armenians, Syrians and Jacobites', as heretics. The dismissal of the Greeks as heretics is so sweeping that it almost certainly referred to the sectarian Paulicians rather than the entire Orthodox community; the letter represents Bohemond's viewpoint and it may have been dictated by him. But when all is said and done, it remains an ominous sign of how things were changing.

There was a natural tendency to associate the ecumenist agenda with the military alliance between the Crusade and Byzantium. So when Alexius's help to the Crusade tailed away almost completely, it encouraged the Crusaders to be sceptical about the Syrian Christians whom they were encountering. These contacts in any case tended towards mutual hostility because of important differences in dogma and worship. For many Crusaders local Christians meant above all the Armenians and Syrians who supplied the Turkish garrison in Antioch, carried out spying missions for the enemy, and took advantage of the famines to sell the Crusaders food at hugely inflated prices. To a large degree the Armenians and Syrians seem to have been neutral in the contest raging around them, though the *GF* contains occasional references to their secret support for the Crusade, as when Christian women in Antioch were observed surreptitiously applauding the deaths of Turks.

A further potent reason for the emergence of a detached and even hostile attitude towards the local Christian churches was the presence on Crusade of many lesser clerics. A large proportion of them were house priests to the *maiores*. These men had little to go back to in the West, but if a Latin (i.e. Catholic) Church was established in Palestine and Syria, they would be the initial beneficiaries. In fact if any single group stood to benefit from the Crusade it was this one, and this must have shaped their attitude. The first such appointment to be made was typical – in October 1098 Raymond of St Gilles appointed one of his priests, Peter of Narbonne, as Bishop of Albara. It is true that Raymond was pro-Byzantine and that Peter was consecrated by the Greek patriarch of Antioch. But a pattern was being established, and Raymond of Aguilers was probably right in his claim that it was a popular one: 'all the people gave thanks to God because they wished to have a Roman bishop in the Eastern Church to look after their affairs.' After the fall of Jerusalem nobody questioned the idea that a Catholic priest would be elected as patriarch, even though the pool of candidates was unpromising: indeed the private life of the man chosen, Arnulf of Chocques, was the subject of bawdy ballads in the army.

It would be a gross exaggeration to say that the First Crusade laid the foundations for a Frankish establishment in the East which was hostile to

8. Engraving of Antioch in the eighteenth century; only the city wall circuit
with bastions survives from the Crusader period.

Byzantium and intolerant of the local Christians. For a variety of reasons that
would have been foolish on military and political grounds as well as need-
lessly retrogressive in terms of the way the upper echelons of the Catholic
Church had approached its relations with the Eastern Churches for the past
thirty years or so. Much would hinge on the way Byzantine relations with
Norman Antioch developed and on the attitudes taken up by settlers and
ecclesiastics arriving from the West. But the trends were not hopeful. It is
tempting to say that the bullishness so evident in the last stage of the expedition can be attributed to the blaze of glory with which (in Latin eyes of
course) the Crusade came to its victorious conclusion. In reality, however,
Latin triumphalism was there from the start. The 'Anonymous' narrates that
while marching through northern Greece, Bohemond's troops encountered
a fortified settlement (*castrum*) containing heretics. What kind of heretics
these were is not stated, but Bohemond's Crusaders stormed their enclosure
and burned them alive. The incident is over in just three sentences, but it
leaves the reader asking questions about juridical authority and mental
outlook which are bound to be awkward.

The massacre of these heretics brings us to the question of how the
Crusaders viewed their Islamic enemies. The 'Anonymous' reveals an

awareness of the basic divide between Seljuqs and Fatimids, describing the former as Turks and the latter as Arabs. But he is not totally consistent, and sometimes these, and other names, are strung together largely in order to make an impression. Thus at Dorylaeum, a battle actually fought against the Seljuq Turks of Anatolia and their allies, he first writes of 'a great multitude of Turks, Arabs, Saracens and other peoples whose names I do not know', later of 'Turks, Arabs, Saracens, Agulani and all the rest of the barbarian nations', and finally of '360,000 Turks, Persians, Paulicians, Saracens and Agulani, with other pagans, not counting the Arabs'. The nomenclature here is as garbled and effect-driven as the arithmetic. Such lists recur: Arqa, for example, was 'full of an immense horde of pagans, Turks, Saracens, Arabs and Paulicians'. The 'Anonymous's' knowledge of Islam is limited and inaccurate, including the common belief that Muslims were polytheistic and that they were encouraged to be gluttonous and lustful.

There were no major obstacles to the Crusaders finding out more about Islam – their army included men, such as an interpreter called Herluin, who spoke Arabic well enough to communicate quite complex demands. Using the services of men like Herluin, the Crusade's leaders negotiated with their opponents, both the Turks and the Fatimids. Aside from religious hostility, there was no insuperable barrier between the armies; in fact the political culture of the Seljuq world in Syria following the deaths of Malik Shah and Nizam al-Mulk, one of fragmentation, unpredictable power shifts and temporary alliances, had much in common with what the Crusaders knew back home. The 'Anonymous' was fairly well-informed on the political situation amongst the Muslims. He was aware of the recent conflicts between the Seljuq Sultan in Iran and the breakaway Seljuqs of western Anatolia, and he knew that Kerbogha's status was that of a provincial governor, appointed at Baghdad and answerable to the Sultan there. It was the will, not the means that was lacking for religious education. The sequences in which Muslims make an appearance in the *GF*, notably the fictitious dialogue between Kerbogha and his mother and al-Afdal's soliloquy of lament after his defeat at Ascalon, feature them merely as puppets, voicing sentiments and ideas which were largely intended to reflect well on the Crusaders. Some local detail is included, but only enough to give these passages the credibility needed to serve their purpose. They resemble manuscript illuminations which show Muslims wearing Frankish armour, and using Western fighting techniques. An attempt at authenticity could have been made (and some illustrators did portray the Muslims differently): the fact that it was not demonstrates a fundamental lack of interest.

For most Crusaders labels sufficed – the Turks were 'enemies of God and holy Christendom'; like German soldiers in old war movies, they were there to be killed. Yet this generalization is not quite accurate, for two different reasons, which somewhat confusingly pull in contradictory directions. First, it can be argued that there were episodes in the Crusade which show that the Muslims were viewed, albeit briefly and selectively, as human beings. To begin with, there was sex. In an expedition on this scale there were inevitably incidents like that of the unnamed nun from Trier, captured during the destruction of Peter the Hermit's army, who was seduced by a Turk and later ran off with her lover. There were Muslim as well as Christian camp-followers. In Stephen of Valence's vision Christ complained that the Crusaders were 'satisfying your filthy lusts both with Christians and with loose pagan women'. The strait-laced Raymond of Aguilers claimed that the Crusaders missed the chance to take Antioch's citadel because 'pagan dancing girls' diverted them. More than enough outrage on this score was expressed by the clerical chroniclers for us to be sure that the sexual attraction of the novel (especially the ethnically novel) sometimes overrode religious hatred. This was not invariably so though: one of the most chilling comments made on the entire Crusade must be Fulcher of Chartres's remark on the looting of Kerbogha's camp by the victorious Crusaders: 'The Franks did no other harm to the women whom they found in the tents, save that they ran their lances through their bellies.'

More importantly, there was a recognition in the last stage of the Crusade of the desirability of converting the Muslims to Christianity. It is well-reflected in the *GF:* Raymond of St Gilles declined to come to an agreement with the Emir of Tripoli unless the latter accepted baptism; eventually the Emir agreed, cannily making it conditional on the Crusaders' success in taking Jerusalem and defeating al-Afdal's army. There was at least one instance of forced conversion, at Tall Mannas, where Muslim peasants who refused baptism were killed. Like prostitution, such a choice of course does not reflect much of a softening of attitude, but overall this intrusion into the Crusade of the theme of conversion represents a crack in the edifice of outright condemnation. The enemy were at least considered as potential converts rather than potential corpses.

The most notable indication that the Turks were considered as human beings rather than as agents of the devil comes in a famous passage in the *GF* in which the 'Anonymous' reviewed the victory at Dorylaeum. The Turks, he commented, were undoubtedly fine warriors, who in the recent past had defeated such opponents as the Greeks, Arabs and Armenians. 'They have a saying that they are of common stock with the Franks, and that no man, except the Franks and themselves, are naturally born to be knights.' And it was true that if they would only become Christians, 'you could not find stronger or braver or more skilful soldiers'. The passage is certainly interesting, not least because, if correct, it shows some sort of dialogue taking place. It is very similar to a comment made on an individual Moorish warrior in *The Song of Roland*, which was written not long afterwards. But such grudging respect is a familiar topos in armed encounters between cultures where military values were in the ascendant: and praise for a defeated enemy is of course a roundabout form of self-congratulation.

These various examples really show us nothing more than that a conflict of this intensity, fought over a protracted period of time, was bound to produce a few shards of curiosity and respect. And they have to be balanced against the reverse phenomenon: the dehumanization of the Muslims. There are two instances of this which call for comment, cannibalism and the massacre at Jerusalem. Both present considerable problems of interpretation. Cannibalism is a complex subject, and it is questionable whether anything should be read into the fact that Turkish bodies were consumed other than an understandable desire to spare the sensitivities of fellow-Crusaders. There is evidence for the existence of a body of poor called the 'Tafurs' who had their own king and gloried in their cannibalization of the enemy's dead. The problem is that the evidence is not strong enough to reach any firm conclusions on the 'Tafurs', let alone to argue as some have tried to do, that their consumption of Muslim flesh had any religious or cultural connotations.

With the massacre at Jerusalem we are on firmer ground, though difficulties remain, due above all to the extreme scarcity of contemporary Muslim sources. The massacre was not unprecedented. At Antioch 'all the streets of the city on every side were full of corpses, so that no-one could endure to be there because of the stench, nor could anyone walk along the narrow paths of the city except over the corpses of the dead'. And at Ma'arrat-an-Numan 'no corner of the city was clear of Saracen corpses, and one could scarcely go about the city streets except by treading on the dead bodies of the Saracens'. Like Jerusalem, these cities were taken by assault; so their populations had no legal right to be spared. As in many instances in warfare in the West, massacre played a cathartic role after the stress of storming the walls. It is important to remember that both at Antioch and at Jerusalem this stress was heightened by the Crusaders' awareness that an enemy relief army was approaching. Yet the slaughter at Jerusalem differed in two respects from events earlier in the Crusade. First, if we accept the testimony of the Western sources it was more extensive. Raymond of

Aguilers commented on the sheer brutality which he witnessed, on the piles of heads, hands and feet which could be seen in the city's streets, and on the ferocious slaughter which took place on the Temple Mount. Ibn al-Athir later claimed that 70,000 were killed in the al-Aqsa mosque, and even if the real figure was a tenth of that, it was clearly a terrible scene. Women and children were not spared. Setting aside as a biblical quotation Raymond's notorious claim that 'men rode in blood up to their knees and bridle reins', this was still an exceptional event. Comparisons with atrocities like William the Conqueror's 'harrying' of the north of England do not take into account the concentrated nature of the slaughter in Jerusalem. Dispassionate as always, the 'Anonymous' remarked that because of the health hazard, the surviving Muslims were given the job of dragging the numerous corpses onto pyramidal mounds 'as big as houses' to be incinerated. Photographs of such mounds taken in Dresden and Hiroshima in 1945 give us some idea of how it must have looked, the difference being that the deaths in Jerusalem were all inflicted by hand. The 'Anonymous' wrote of the Crusaders 'thirsting and craving for the blood of the Turks' and in Jerusalem they slaked their thirst.

The massacre at Jerusalem also had a religious meaning. As a massive release of stress, it stemmed from the same psychological roots as the excitement and joy which the Crusaders manifested within the church of the Holy Sepulchre. But the two actions had more than psychology in common. They both sprang from what one historian recently described as the 'overwhelming spirit of righteousness' with which the siege and capture of Jerusalem were conducted. The holy places were being purged as well as being liberated, and the massacre was perceived as a necessary cleansing. It was not something to disguise or regret: in the newsletter which the Crusade's leaders sent to the new Pope, Paschal II, in September 1099, they made specific reference to the carnage which had recently been perpetrated on the Temple Mount. Raymond of Aguilers wrote that 'it was a just and splendid judgement of God that this place should be filled with the blood of the unbelievers, since it had suffered so long from their blasphemies'. In broad terms, the bloodshed was mandated by God and it constituted the culmination of the Crusade's overall programme. It was also a deeply eschatological act, for contemporaries were quick to see much significance in the fact that Jerusalem fell on 15 July, the day associated with the apostles' departure from the city to preach the faith throughout the world. The play of ideas at work here constituted a danger similar to linking the Crusade with vendetta, for it was tantamount to declaring that the actual shedding of blood (rather than the goals achieved through its shedding, something very different) constituted a God-pleasing act, maybe even one which was in itself holy. It is hard to imagine a more perilous concept to introduce to a society which was already permeated by martial values. It was to have a very long life: when Portuguese Crusaders captured Ceuta in 1415, Prince Henry 'The Navigator' complained that he had not yet had the chance to kill any Moors. How could he be dubbed as a knight 'if my sword has not been dipped to the hilt in the blood of the infidels?'

As we saw at the start of the chapter, the Muslims would not forget or forgive the events of July 1099. Yet in a curious way their role in the massacre was incidental to its genesis. There can have been few victims who were less guilty than the Muslims of Jerusalem, or indeed possessed less sense of why they and their families were being butchered. The massacre was another consequence of the package of ideas which constituted penitential warfare, and its roots lay deep in the specific ways Western society had evolved since the break up of the Roman empire. No more than the Byzantines could the Muslims hope to comprehend the Crusaders. Even the closest idea Islam has to crusading, that of *jihad*, was at a low ebb at this point. Writing more than a century later, Ibn al-Athir fell back on a broad perspective, which linked the First Crusade to recent episodes of Christian aggression against Islam in the Mediterranean world, the fall of Toledo in 1085 and the Norman invasion of Sicily in 1091. This made at least as much sense as Anna Comnena's view of the Crusade, or Crusader views of the Muslim political world. It is clear that the arrival of the crusading armies struck the whole Middle East with the force of a bolt of lightning, and that both Byzantine Greeks and Muslims fumbled to make sense of a military scenario which had been thrown into utter confusion. As the dust settled they would begin to form an understanding of the strengths and limitations of the Latin states which had been established during the Crusade or in its aftermath. What they could not predict was the arrival of fresh armies of Crusaders from the West, their size, make-up and destination. For the next three centuries this would form their recurrent dilemma.

2

VILLEHARDOUIN'S 'LA CONQUÊTE DE CONSTANTINOPLE': CRUSADING AND CONQUEST

The decades which followed the capture of Jerusalem in 1099 present us with a paradox. There is no evidence that Urban II planned that the armed pilgrimage would be a recurrent feature of devotional life in the West or that taking the Cross would become an institution in the liturgical and legal senses. The group of Benedictine monks who were the most sophisticated chroniclers of the First Crusade celebrated its uniqueness. Yet for a number of reasons it was soon apparent that what had happened in the East could not be regarded as an unrepeatable event in Christian history. At the same time that Western contemporaries were struggling to conceptualize what had taken place, circumstances dictated that there would have to be more such expeditions. In the first place, the new settlements in Palestine and Syria needed all the help they could get from the West. The comparatively few Crusaders who remained in Palestine and Syria faced the two-fold task of conquering the string of coastal towns that could be used by the Fatimids of

Egypt to disembark sea-borne armies and of repelling counter-attacks launched from the towns of the Seljuq interior, especially Damascus, Aleppo and Mosul. There was naturally a wave of enthusiasm to take the Cross on the part of people who had failed to respond in 1095–6 or who had reached maturity since. The association of crusading with pilgrimage remained overwhelmingly strong. It was not necessary to wait for a papal proclamation or a preaching campaign to take the Cross – individuals did so in much the same way that they decided to embark on pilgrimage, as a personal decision taken largely for devotional reasons. Others came East as pilgrims, but agreed to take up arms on arrival to help the hard-pressed settlers, effectively becoming Crusaders on the spot. This probably applied to King Sigurd of Norway, whose fleet reached Palestine in 1110; he was persuaded to assist King Baldwin I of Jerusalem in taking the port of Sidon. At the same time Urban II's successors adhered to the approach he had laid down, that the Spanish *Reconquista* should also be treated as a crusading arena. The full remission of sins granted by Urban II in 1095 was offered to knights who fought against the Moors, their most notable success being the Aragonese conquest of Zaragoza in 1118.

But it was the East which held the attention of twelfth-century Christendom: one reason for extending the Crusade to Spain was the anxiety felt by the churchmen there that their best fighters would be lured away by the Holy Land. From the 1140s onwards the pride felt at Jerusalem being once more in Christian hands was enhanced by returning pilgrims who told friends and relatives about the impressive building programmes which were under way. This applied above all to the church of the Holy Sepulchre. The Byzantine rotunda sheltering Christ's tomb was extended to encompass a substantial nave, while large-scale conventual facilities were built for the church's twenty canons. Christendom's holiest shrines, Calvary, the site where Christ's body was anointed, and the tomb itself were all held within a Romanesque structure, which was celebrated as one of the marvels of the age. It also contained the tombs of the kings of Jerusalem, a reminder to visiting pilgrims that the rich devotional experience they were enjoying depended on the fragile carapace of Frankish power.

Not surprisingly therefore, it was serious military defeat which led to important crusading ventures, through the mechanism of appeals to the Pope and great lords in the West. Just as during the First Crusade itself, the Franks depended on the prevalence of political and religious disunity amongst their Muslim enemies to survive; any movement towards Islamic unity was highly dangerous to them. So too was any advocacy of *jihad*,

Islamic holy war, which was usually associated with an appeal for unity. It was in circumstances of *jihad* that the Franks suffered their first major defeat in the East, when Roger of Antioch was killed at the luridly named battle of the Field of Blood in 1119. Desperate appeals to the West persuaded Pope Calixtus II to take vigorous action, calling for a simultaneous Crusade in Palestine and Spain. The most conspicuous outcome of Calixtus's appeal was the dispatch eastward of a Venetian fleet of 100 vessels commanded by the Doge in person. This expedition of 1122–5 was the most substantial Venetian contribution to the Crusades to date and it bears some resemblance to the Fourth Crusade: the fleet and army were both large, they were led by the Doge and they embarked after an enthusiastic display of religious fervour in St Mark's, which was already established as the venue for large-scale civic occasions. The Venetians spent the winter of 1122–3 on Byzantine Corfu, ravaging the island as a means of putting pressure on the Emperor to be more compliant in trading negotiations which were underway. When they did reach the Holy Land they played a crucial role in conquering Tyre, one of the most important ports, in exchange for a handsome portfolio of commercial privileges. On their way back home, they inflicted further damage on Byzantine islands in the Aegean. Undeniably a case can be made for this Crusade serving the purposes of Venetian trade, but to regard the Venetian involvement as devoid of religious motivation would entail divorcing the republic from the mainstream of twelfth-century devotional feelings. A better way to characterize Venetian attitudes, on this occasion, as later, would be to recognize that a city which depended on trade to survive had to ensure that all its major public undertakings were in harmony with its commercial needs. Venice could not afford the luxury of a large-scale military outlay that did not offer a return.

If this seems shocking it shows only that we are regarding crusading motivation in the wrong light, as an either/or issue. The surgical isolation of religious motivation in this way is wholly unrealistic, like cutting the heart from the body and expecting it to survive. Two comparisons may help. As is well known, the Franks in Palestine and Syria did not conduct their affairs in an atmosphere of unrelenting holy war. In a broad perspective they did view their presence in the Holy Land in religious terms, as part of a divine plan. This is epitomized by the chronicle of Latin Syria's greatest historian, William of Tyre. At important military encounters the knights of the kingdom of Jerusalem marched behind their greatest relic, the portion of the True Cross which had been discovered in 1099 – primarily it was believed to throw a supernatural shield over them, but it was also a pointer towards their rationale. In their day-to-day dealings with Aleppo and Damascus, however, the settlers normally aimed at a *modus vivendi*, adhering to a pattern of regional coalitions, which took realistic account of their own position and the strengths and weaknesses of their Muslim neighbours. At times this approach shocked visiting Crusaders, but it was inevitable.

The second comparison is with Pope Calixtus II. The Pope's response to the disaster of 1119 sprang primarily from his consciousness of his position as head of Christendom. But he was also aware that this exertion of authority would prove beneficial in his difficult dealings with the Western Emperor. Throughout the central Middle Ages popes and emperors had inherently volatile relationships, which were bound to impinge on papal attitudes towards the Crusade. And Calixtus was not least conscious of his personal obligations, because as one of his letters pointed out, the Pope was related to King Baldwin II of Jerusalem. It is striking that while the Franks suffered their defeat of 1119 in northern Syria, the events of Calixtus's Crusade played themselves out in Palestine, far to the south. So even this reassertion of papal authority over the Crusade, following several years of relative inertia, was conditioned by the kinship ties that had proved so prominent in generating and mobilizing the initial crusading enthusiasm of 1095–99.

In broad terms, the capture of Tyre did compensate for the battle of the Field of Blood. It clinched Frankish control over the coast, robbing the Fatimids of their last port north of Jerusalem and bringing the Venetians into a network of commercial activity and naval support which already included their rivals: the Genoese and Pisans. But the situation in the northern states was much more difficult. Here the Franks suffered the consequences of the first movement towards Islamic unity, the incorporation of Aleppo into Mosul's sphere of influence. In 1144 the governor of Mosul, 'Imad al-Din Zengi, took the city of Edessa and all but destroyed the first of the states established by the First Crusade. The Pope, Eugenius III, responded with an impressive encyclical calling for a Crusade, *Quantum praedecessores*, but it was St Bernard of Clairvaux who built up the momentum for what became the Second Crusade through the effectiveness of his preaching and the force of his personality. His most important recruits were Kings Louis VII of France and Conrad III of Germany, who led armies through the Balkans and into Anatolia. The result was catastrophic. In October 1147 Conrad's army suffered a horrific defeat near the site of the battle of Dorylaeum of 1097. The French army fared almost as badly at Mount Cadmus in January 1148. The survivors made their way to Palestine by sea, and in June 1148 it was decided that the remnants of both forces would combine with the army of

King Baldwin III of Jerusalem in besieging Damascus. Given the losses sustained in Anatolia this shift in goals to consolidating the situation in the south rather than trying to regain Edessa made good sense, but the siege of Damascus was poorly conducted and failed. Louis and Conrad sailed home from Acre with nothing to show for their massive efforts.

The Second Crusade was probably the broadest in scope of any of the Crusades. Like Urban II and Calixtus II before him, Eugenius III had been persuaded to extend the Crusade to include fighting in Spain. But there was more: the Danes and Saxons successfully lobbied for their attacks on the pagan Wends in Pomerania to be accorded Crusade status. There was considerable naval activity, most importantly taking the form of a north-European fleet, which assisted the Portuguese in seizing Lisbon before proceeding eastward. But this and similar gains in Iberia could not balance the loss of both the French and German armies in the East. The defeat of the initial wave of the First Crusade and of the follow-up armies in 1101 had been submerged in the glory of 1099. The mood in the years following 1148, by contrast, was entirely sombre, not to say desperate. The two leading commentators on what had happened, Otto of Freising and St Bernard, both attempted to explain the disaster in terms of the inscrutability of God's will and the sinful behaviour of the Crusaders. Both became standard approaches towards crusading failure, but while they satisfied theologians they were much less acceptable to the laity. Ordinary Christians sought refuge in apathy. For almost forty years crusading appeals from the popes, mainly generated in response to embassies and letters from the Latin East, fell on stony ground.

The Second Crusade bequeathed two further legacies of significance. One was suspicion of the Byzantine Greeks. Louis VII had gone East with a generally wary attitude towards the Emperor Manuel Comnenus, but Conrad III had been in alliance with Manuel against the Normans of southern Italy. The route they both took, more or less following in the footsteps of Godfrey of Bouillon, placed them in the same position at Constantinople as the leaders of the First Crusade. They needed supplies and vessels to cross the Bosporus, while Manuel placed a priority on keeping the imperial capital safe while exacting oaths that any former Byzantine lands which the Crusaders managed to capture would be returned to him. Relations soured much as they had in 1097, and a virulently anti-Byzantine faction in Louis's army, led by Godfrey, Bishop of Langres, advocated storming Constantinople to make Manuel see sense. The city, he claimed, was 'Christian only in name'. The situation got worse in Anatolia, where promised Greek supplies failed to appear and Byzantine garrisons took no action when the Turks attacked the

Crusaders. Louis VII returned with bitter feelings towards Manuel and he even planned a new Crusade which, like the Venetians in 1122–3, would start by attacking Byzantine lands.

The other legacy of the Second Crusade was a crystallization of ideas about the status of Crusaders, the validity of what they were doing, and how their efforts could best be organized. Although not the first papal encyclical for a Crusade, *Quantum praedecessores* was a keystone document. It set out clearly some of the basic privileges enjoyed by those who took the Cross: Church protection for their families and property during their absence, exemption from paying interest on debts, and the postponement of any court cases in which they were involved. Such privileges evolved from those that had traditionally been granted to pilgrims but in the case of Crusaders they became more extensive. Papal *auctoritas* was being exerted, and it helped that St Bernard deferred to the Pope *ex officio*, even though his personal standing was much higher – Eugenius was in fact a former pupil. Just as significant as *Quantum praedecessores* was a text which had appeared a few years previously, Gratian's *Decretum*. Gratian was an academic lawyer, his *Decretum* the first systematic compilation of Church or canon law. The Crusade was not yet advanced enough as an institution to require separate treatment but Gratian devoted a whole section (*Causa* 23) to the consideration of what made a conflict just. From this point onward anybody reflecting on the Church's involvement in warfare, which obviously included crusading, would include within their argument Gratian's careful analysis of the conditions under which wars could lawfully be waged by the Church.

Few Crusaders read *Quantum praedecessores* or had heard of Gratian, but many churchmen with whom they came into contact did and had. When the north European crusading fleet reached Portugal the Bishop of Oporto apparently used a series of ingenious legal arguments to persuade the Crusaders that it was fully in keeping with their goals to assist in the siege of Lisbon. There was sensitivity too on the issue of organization. Individuals continued to go to the East on what have been described as 'personal mini-Crusades', especially when their social standing was high enough for them to take a household with them. But increasingly monarchs were expected to provide leadership, especially the kings of France and England, and the Holy Roman Emperor. The disasters of the Second Crusade destroyed the fixation on aping the First Crusade which had largely been responsible for the loss of the German and French armies. Once marine technology had reached the stage at which large bodies of men, together with their horses and equipment, could be transported over long distances, the advantages of going

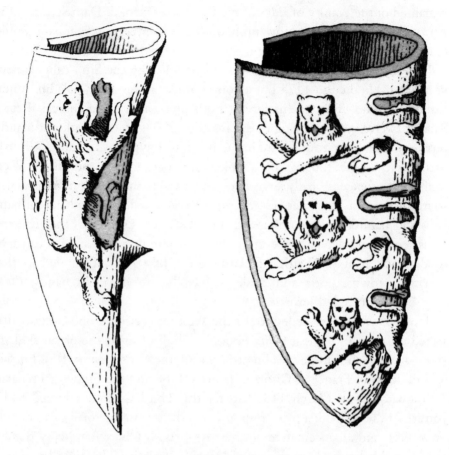

9. and 10. Arms of Richard I.

East by sea became obvious. Eudes of Deuil, the leading chronicler of Louis VII's expedition, condemned the large numbers of unarmed pilgrims who held up progress and consumed precious supplies, 'the defenceless mob, which has always harmed us and on whose account food is more expensive and progress slower'. The military logic was to exclude them completely, and while it would not fully achieve this, travelling by sea would clearly keep out those who could not even afford their passage.

As long as papal appeals for a Crusade met with little or no response, these considerations remained largely theoretical. What changed things, once again, was a military disaster in the East, and this time it was one which thoroughly dwarfed the events of 1119 and 1144. After the failure of the siege of Damascus in 1148 the movement towards Islamic unity was continued by Zengi's son Nur al-Din. Operating from Aleppo, he wiped out what remained of the county of Edessa, and he took control of Damascus in 1154. All of Muslim Syria was now unified, with an increasing emphasis on the practice of *jihad* and especially on the reconquest of Jerusalem. In 1169 Nur al-Din also brought Egypt under his rule, abolishing the Shi'i caliphate two years later. He died in 1174 but a young officer in his army, Saladin, immediately staked a claim to his legacy, both political and ideological. It took Saladin twelve years to bring under his control the whole swathe of Muslim territory stretching from Mosul in the north to Egypt in the south. While he was doing so he fought the Franks only occasionally, but in 1187 he mobilized an exceptionally large army and invaded the kingdom of Jerusalem south of the Sea of Galilee. Common sense dictated the avoidance of battle in such hazardous circumstances, but Guy of Lusignan, the King of Jerusalem, assembled almost every fighting man in his realm and led this army to destruction at the battle of Hattin on 4 July 1187. Denuded of their garrisons, towns, ports and castles fell easily into Saladin's hands. On 2 October he occupied Jerusalem.

This was what was needed to stir the West into action. Pope Gregory VIII issued a call to Crusade, *Audita tremendi*, a bull of great rhetorical skill. All three of Western Europe's leading rulers took the Cross, Henry II of England and Philip II of France at Gisors in January 1188 and the Emperor Frederick I ('Barbarossa') in March 1188. So far the Third Crusade adhered to the pattern of the Second: a papal response to a disaster in the form of a powerful encyclical, and an acceptance on the part of both Church and laity that the armies needed would be organized by the monarchs. This time there were no other crusading fronts, all efforts being required just to recover Jerusalem. But Europe's monarchs brought their politics with them, and the planning of the Anglo-French expedition was held up by Henry II's disputes with his eldest son, Richard the Lionheart. Henry's death in July 1189 brought Richard to the throne and, assembling at Vézelay in Burgundy, the English and French Crusaders began their march to the Mediterranean coast on the third anniversary of Hattin, 4 July 1190. Richard embarked his troops at Marseilles and Philip at Genoa.

Travelling by sea released the English and French armies from the clogging effect of a mass of unarmed pilgrims, and it freed them from having to negotiate with the Byzantines and from crossing Anatolia in the teeth of Turkish opposition. But it brought with it other problems, the most important being the strong possibility of delay and diversion. Richard's voyage to Palestine illustrates this well. He wintered at Messina in Sicily and became embroiled in dynastic politics, which led him to sack Messina itself.

11. A page from the thirteenth-century manuscript 'Itinerarium of King Richard Coeur-de-Lion'. The writer enters into minute particulars of the Third Crusade and claims to have been present with Richard in Palestine – a medieval 'war correspondent' in fact. The following is a translation of a passage describing the character of the King: 'He [King Richard I] certainly was of noble bearing and was a fine figure of a man. His hair neither red nor golden but half-way between the two; his limbs were straight and supple; his arms somewhat elongated, which came in very handy for the drawing of the sword and which rendered him a useful man at wielding it: to harmonise, his legs were also long and his whole noble bodily proportions were to match. His appearance was that of one born to rule, whose fitness to do so was due in no small degree to his refinement and bearing. The general recognition of these great qualities he earned not by the noble birth alone but by the virtues that were his adornment.'

Proceeding eastward in April 1191, he invaded Cyprus and conquered the island from a Greek nobleman, Isaac Comnenus, who had made the mistake of imprisoning some of the English Crusaders. The nature of Richard's Sicilian and Cypriot campaigns should not be misconstrued. They were affairs of honour and prestige rather than simple adventures and both were justifiable in legal terms. But they do show the way in which travel by sea encouraged the inherent tendency for Crusades to the East to splinter and fragment. This tendency was further stimulated by the process of internal dissolution, which was overtaking the Byzantine empire at this point; Isaac Comnenus was effectively independent of the government at Constantinople when he faced English invasion in 1191.

If there were potential dangers in going by sea, it was still preferable to the notorious hazards of the land route, and these were demonstrated anew by the fate of the German army on the Third Crusade. Frederick Barbarossa did not really have the option of going by sea, but having witnessed the chaos of the Second Crusade as a young man, he did his best to alert and reassure the rulers of lands which he planned to pass through. These included the Byzantines and the Seljuq Sultan of Iconium. The latter was no friend of Saladin, whereas the Byzantine Emperor Isaac Angelus had gone so far as to enter an alliance with him. The German army stalled outside Constantinople in the autumn of 1189 and in November Frederick wrote to his son Henry asking him to organize Italian naval assistance for a siege of the city in the spring of 1190. This did not prove necessary: the Crusaders were allowed to cross at the Dardanelles and their march across Anatolia was executed with relative smoothness. Then came the death of Barbarossa in a swimming accident in June 1190, a bizarre event which thoroughly broke German morale and reduced their contribution to the Crusade to a shadow of what it would have been under the Emperor's leadership.

Once they had fully assembled in Palestine in the summer of 1191, the Crusaders achieved much greater successes than the Second Crusade had enjoyed. There was a clear military objective in the siege of Acre, the most important of the ports which had fallen to Saladin in the wake of Hattin. Acre was occupied by the Crusaders on 12 July and Philip II, who felt himself overshadowed both militarily and politically by the English King, sailed home soon afterwards. Richard remained to inflict an impressive defeat on Saladin at the battle of Arsur in September 1191; but his two attempts to march inland and take Jerusalem, at the end of 1191 and in June 1192, both had to be abandoned in the face of the severe logistical difficulties involved. In September English envoys agreed on a truce with Saladin, which

puſo me oracio ſoacio ſeo unte meſe: ſi
cain ſeo ſuſſeptoſ meus es.

12. Richard and Saladin represented in the Luttrell Psalter.

confirmed the Christian hold on the coast from Tyre to Jaffa and guaranteed both Christians and Muslims free passage through Palestine. With Richard's departure from Acre in October 1192 the Crusade came to an end.

A century after Urban II's proclamation of the First Crusade in 1095, both crusading and the strategic situation in the Latin East presented fascinating and complex profiles. In both cases there was strength and fragility, forces and mechanisms that were creative but at the same time interests and contradictions which proved inherently fissile and destructive. Taking the Latin East first, the dominant impression left by the Third Crusade was of an agenda which had been incompletely realized. Saladin's death in 1193 removed some of the pressure from the Franks, and German Crusaders who arrived in 1197 added Sidon and Beirut to the group of ports which were in the hands of the Franks. But they still lacked Jerusalem, were dangerously confined to the coastal littoral and faced encirclement by their Muslim enemies. It was a situation that demanded innovative thinking. Ever since Nur al-Din had extended his power to Egypt in the 1160s, it had been apparent that the heartland of Muslim strength ('the serpent's head') was the fertile Nile Delta and that the most effective way to drive off a threat to Palestine, and even to

Syria, was to launch an invasion of Egypt. Richard I had given serious thought to this during the Third Crusade. The conquest of Egypt, a dream of the Crusaders since the arrival of the First Crusade, would be the best solution. Failing that, it might be possible to trade territorial gains made in Egypt for an extension of the coastal perimeter to include Jerusalem. This new strategic approach was only possible because of the dominance over the Mediterranean seaways, which had been won during the twelfth century by the Italian trading republics. It enabled the crusading armies which they carried to strike with impunity at any point they wanted, with the added advantage of surprise provided the destination was kept secret. The weakness of the Christian grip on the Holy Land, obvious from any map of their holdings, was to some extent compensated by this development – the fact that Cyprus, seized by Richard I in 1191, remained in Latin Christian hands thereafter for almost four centuries, was very largely due to the West's unchallenged control of the sea.

The wild card in the strategic scenario was Byzantium. It is remarkable that the Eastern empire passed from being the firm (if unreliable) ally of the Crusaders during the First Crusade, via countless misunderstandings and disenchantments, to siding with their Muslim opponents at the time of the Third Crusade. Byzantine alienation from the idea of Crusade meant that they had a very limited understanding of how reprehensible this seemed to Catholics; to the Greeks it was simply diplomacy. Over much the same period the Italian trading powers came to view the Byzantine empire as a fickle and at times treacherous commercial partner. Confronted by a host of problems, which included provincial separatism, economic decline and military defeat, the emperors had no option but to implement harsh fiscal policies. When these caused popular unrest in Constantinople, it was all too easy for the court to make use of the anti-Latin resentment to channel it into rioting against resident Italian traders. In 1171 Venetian merchants within the empire were purged, and in 1182 there was a massacre of the Latins in Constantinople. Had it been pursued, Barbarossa's decision in 1189 to raise a fleet in Italy for an assault on Constantinople would have met with a warm welcome at Venice. In the meantime there was little movement either on the Latin or on the Greek side towards reconciling their differences in religious doctrine and liturgical practice. There were thus a number of powerful currents of antagonism towards the Greeks in the West in the 1190s. It would be rash to generalize, but it is certainly safe to say that the Byzantine empire's image in the West was poor; it had many enemies and few friends.

As for crusading, it was clearly in the throes of major change. The days of the armed pilgrimage were past. After Barbarossa's death no army took the overland route across the Balkans for two centuries; the geo-political scenario would be transformed before it was followed again. The military capabilities of the English army commanded by Richard the Lionheart had shown what could be achieved when an administrative machinery of proven worth was allowed to handle the assembly and payment of a Crusade. It was clear that such forces, transported by sea, their disembarkation timed to coincide with the ending of a truce between the Franks and the Muslims, represented the most effective way to combat the enemy. But there were numerous problems involved. The dependence on secular government had to be reconciled with the Pope's role as the initiator of Crusades and with the Church's responsibility in preaching them. Increasingly the issue of who should pay for Crusades loomed large. In both England and France the Third Crusade had been financed by taxing the whole community through what became known as 'the Saladin tithe'. It was bitterly resented and could not be done again. In addition, if crusading was not to be associated directly with pilgrimage to Jerusalem and worship at its shrines, then its nature and value as a penitential act had to be made clear.

Such a situation called for a man of vision and determination and one was elected Pope in 1198. Lothario dei Conti di Segni, who took the name Innocent III, saw the plight of the Holy Land as one of his most pressing concerns. At no point did he merely pay it lip service, which makes all the more significant his readiness to declare Crusades in other theatres of operation. Most previous popes had described themselves as vicars of St Peter, but Innocent preferred, and exploited to the full, the alternative title of Vicar of Christ. This placed on his shoulders a particular obligation to promote what was often termed 'Christ's business' (*negotium Christi*), and it made him willing to adopt a more interventionist stance than any previous pope had done. This entailed accepting financial responsibility, which Innocent argued should be shared by the whole Church in its spiritual capacity as Christ's bride. Above all Innocent wanted Crusades to succeed. The word efficacy (*efficacia*) occurs frequently in his voluminous correspondence. It meant attention to detail at every stage, from planning and initiation through to arrangements for campaigning; and it applied not least to the organizing of a programme of penitential and intercessory activities to take place throughout the Catholic world while a Crusade was in progress.

This was the background to the Fourth Crusade, which Innocent proclaimed in August 1198. It is worth emphasizing that this was the first major expedition since Urban II's not to be summoned in response to news of a disaster. The Crusade's leaders would therefore enjoy maximum flexibility in deciding their field of operations, though the expedition's goal was the recovery of Jerusalem. The problem was who these leaders would be. It used to be thought that Innocent III reacted against the royal and imperial leadership of the Second and Third Crusades by reasserting papal control over crusading. This is too straightforward. It is true that the Crusade organized by the Emperor Henry VI, Barbarossa's successor, which was largely aborted after Henry's premature death in 1197, came as close to excluding the Pope as a Crusade could; this set a precedent, which had to be guarded against. It is also the case that Innocent took more practical measures in his Crusade encyclical than any of his predecessors had, and that he expected his legates on the expedition to be proactive and forceful. In December 1199 he took measures to tax the whole Church for the Crusade, which clearly entitled him to expect a measure of control over it. But Innocent was nothing if pragmatic; he would have worked with a monarch if one had offered to take part in the Crusade. Imperial leadership was not to be expected because following Henry VI's death the throne of the Holy Roman empire was contested between Henry's younger brother, Philip of Swabia and Innocent's own *protégé*, Otto of Brunswick. Philip II and Richard I were at war. Philip was not interested in repeating his painful experiences on the Third Crusade and King John, who succeeded Richard in March 1199, regarded the Crusade as a diversion from more pressing matters at home.

A year after Innocent called for his Crusade the results were slender and it seemed possible that his appeal would share the fate of many earlier papal initiatives, which had produced no action. That it did not was probably due to two considerations. The first was the Pope's own persistence, not least his decision to tax the Church, which probably allayed the anxiety of many about how the costs of a crusading commitment would be met. The second was the fact that the European generation which reached maturity around 1190 was exposed to the appeal of crusading more fully than any other before or after. The Third Crusade only ended in 1192, and Henry VI's Crusade in 1197. Pope Celestine III issued Crusade encyclicals for Spain in 1193 and 1197, and both Celestine and Innocent were generous in granting crusading privileges to the Christians fighting pagans in the Baltic settlement of Livonia. It might be thought that such widespread grants would divert crusading enthusiasm from the needs of the Holy Land, but it is equally likely that they helped sustain an atmosphere of receptivity to the crusading message. Family traditions of participating in Crusades had now become fully developed. Above all, the loss in 1187 of all the shrines of Jerusalem and

Judea continued to be keenly felt. There was a palpable sense of deprivation, almost of grief, focused on the disappearance at Hattin of the relic of the True Cross. It is quite possible that religious sensibilities were as exposed as at the time of Urban II's preaching of the First Crusade.

Towards the end of 1199 these sensibilities finally started to give expression to commitment as high-ranking magnates took the Cross and people lower down the social scale took their cue from them. Effective preaching was essential, and the Fourth Crusade found its St Bernard in a parish priest called Fulk of Neuilly, who combined charismatic preaching with miracle healing. At the centre of Fulk's message was a call to repentance linked to a denunciation of the more conspicuous sins such as avarice and lust. One chronicler wrote of his signing 200,000 people with the Cross. Another, putting the cart before the horse, depicted Innocent's decision to proclaim the Crusade as springing from his admiration for Fulk's success as a preacher. It is more likely that Fulk's preaching during the summer of 1199 created a ripple effect which spread outward from his own circuit in the Île-de-France. One region strongly affected was Champagne, a heartland of crusading. Here, at a tournament held at Écry on 28 November 1199, the counts Thibaut of Champagne and Louis of Blois took the Cross. They were the most important recruits to date, and in February 1200 they were joined by Count Baldwin of Flanders. This brought into the Crusade another region possessing very rich traditions of past crusading.

The meeting at Écry was almost certainly attended by Geoffrey of Villehardouin, Count Thibaut's Marshal. Villehardouin himself took the Cross and in 1207, when the Crusade had ended, he completed a narrative account known as 'The Conquest of Constantinople' (La Conquête de Constantinople, hereafter CdC). It is one of the best-known and most readable of medieval sources and ranks among the earliest prose works written in Old French. Villehardouin was no rank-and-file Crusader. Born in the early 1150s to a well-connected noble family, he had been Marshal since 1185. He was an experienced soldier, counsellor and administrator. He played a central role in almost every major set of negotiations conducted during the Fourth Crusade and was obviously held in high esteem by the expedition's leaders. Perhaps his finest hour came in the summer of 1204 when he was entrusted with healing a breach of relations between Baldwin of Flanders and Boniface of Montferrat which looked set to destroy the fragile Frankish establishment in Thrace. In this capacity, 'speaking as a privileged friend', he even took it upon himself to rebuke Boniface for his behaviour. He died about ten years after completing his history.

13. Route taken by the Fourth Crusade.

Villehardouin was a supporter of the series of diversions that took the Fourth Crusade to Constantinople and personally benefited from them: he became Marshal of the Latin empire of Constantinople, which was proclaimed after the city's fall to the Crusaders. This naturally makes us highly wary of his assertion that he wrote nothing but the truth. The *CdC* is not propaganda or even, in the strict sense, an 'official history' of the Crusade. Probably the best way to characterize it is as a veteran soldier's record for posterity of remarkable events, in which he knew that he had played a crucial role and felt that he could give the most reliable account. Luckily it is usually possible to check Villehardouin's version of events against that offered by others. In particular there is an almost full history of the Crusade by Robert of Cléry, another eyewitness and an ordinary knight from Picardy with no axe to grind. By such means Villehardouin has been cleared of fabrication and even of serious distortion. But he does occasionally omit important events or make light of them, and there is no doubt that the *CdC* conveys a message: that the diversions of the Crusade arose from circumstances rather than from conspiracy, that these diversions were necessary in order to preserve the army intact, and that the Crusade's achievement in conquering Constantinople was both providential and glorious.

Villehardouin's history is far from the annals tradition favoured by monastic chroniclers, in which events are firmly anchored chronologically. He provided so few dates that the reconstruction of events becomes very difficult when there are no other sources to bring to bear. In keeping with the office which he held, his history reads rather like a series of military dispatches, not least because of his penchant for praising the feats of individual knights and recording the deaths of notable members of the army. The flavour of the battlefield, siege-works and camp is direct, enhanced by rich and credible detail and given immediacy by the recreation of speech. At times this latter habit becomes incongruous, as when Villehardouin records the terms offered to the Crusaders by the Venetians in the form of a lengthy speech delivered by the Doge. On the other hand it relieves the *CdC* of any descriptive dryness, achieving the sense of momentum and ceaseless activity which was undoubtedly Villehardouin's aim. His history is, and was intended to be, a 'page turner'. Hence the occasional splashes of rhetorical colour:

> '...let me tell you of one of the most remarkable and extraordi-
> nary events you have ever heard of... never before had so grand
> an enterprise been carried out by any people since the creation
> of the world... let me tell you of an event so marvellous that it
> might be called a miracle'.

Such phrases are reminiscent of the style of the *chansons de geste*, with their concern to keep the audience attentive; and it was a style which suited Villehardouin's conviction that the fate of the Fourth Crusade was shaped by events rather than by human planning.

Because of his position Villehardouin is able to give us an insider's view of how Thibaut of Champagne, Louis of Blois and Baldwin of Flanders handled the problems posed by the absence of royal leadership. Immediately following an impressive roll-call of Crusaders, he describes meetings, which were held in the course of 1200 at Soissons and Compiègne. At Compiègne 'many different forms of advice were given' (one would dearly like to know what they were) and the outcome was the appointment of a group of six plenipotentiaries, including Villehardouin, to make contractual arrangements for vessels to transport the Crusaders to the East. They agreed that Venice was most likely to be able to provide sufficient ships, and crossed the Alps in midwinter to negotiate with the Doge, Enrico Dandolo, in February 1201. By any reckoning Dandolo was an extraordinary man. Nearly eighty years of age when elected Doge in 1193, he must have been close to ninety when he discussed the situation with Villehardouin and his colleagues. Although he was nearly blind, his intellect was crystal clear and his judgement acute, enabling him to make the best use of his own massive experience. His executive power as Doge was not far short of monarchical and he effectively spoke for Venice throughout the Crusade. Dandolo could hardly listen to the crusading envoys without reflecting on Veneto-Byzantine relations: he had been to Constantinople at least twice to negotiate with the Greeks and his personal dislike for them was enshrined in a later story that it was an injury suffered at Greek hands which caused his blindness. His city's trade with Constantinople remained very important and there were thousands of Venetian merchants living there in a precarious manner at this point. Given this situation and Dandolo's calibre as a diplomat, it is obvious that he saw possibilities opening up. It is easy to see why some historians have argued for a Venetian conspiracy to divert the Crusade being hatched at this early stage, and for this very reason it must be emphasized that there is not a shred of evidence for it.

Given subsequent events, it is not surprising that the terms, which Dandolo offered to the plenipotentiaries, have received a good deal of attention. The Venetians would provide transport for an army of 4,500 knights, an equal number of mounts, 9,000 squires and 20,000 foot soldiers, together with provisions for a full year. The prices which were eventually agreed on were four marks of silver for each knight and two marks for each horse, squire and foot soldier, making a total of 85,000 silver marks of Cologne weight. This sum should be paid by April 1202, and the Crusade would set sail on 29 June 1202. In comparison with contracts made a few years earlier the Venetian terms were quite high but by no means exorbitant. The problem was the very large number of Crusaders for whom transport would be provided, because the sum of 85,000 marks due was fixed, irrespective of how many Crusaders were ready to embark when the time came. Why the baronial envoys thought it necessary to plan for an army of well over 30,000 men remains baffling. These numbers were much larger than those led East by Richard I and Philip II, and at the Soissons conference concern had been expressed about the slowness of recruitment. As one historian of the Crusade recently put it, the envoys were being 'extravagantly optimistic, to say the least'. One can only assume that they anticipated an acceleration in recruitment once the news of the departure date became generally known; perhaps they also thought that if a shortfall in numbers did occur, the proceeds from the Pope's taxation of the Church would be available to help pay the bill.

14. Château Gaillard, Richard the Lionheart's great fortress castle overlooking the River Seine to the east of Rouen. Familiarity with besieging castles on this scale equipped the Crusaders well for their siege of Constantinople.

Villehardouin's account of the negotiations at Venice is not very helpful on these issues. His tone is one of satisfaction at the success enjoyed by the envoys in arranging guaranteed shipping on this scale and relief at Dandolo's ability to persuade his people to assist the Crusade. Regrettably no contemporary Venetian account exists to control Villehardouin's colourful description of the scenes of lachrymose emotion in St Mark's when Dandolo brought the negotiations to the attention of the Venetian popular assembly (*arengo*). Here, in 'the most beautiful church in the world', Villehardouin himself appealed to the Venetians to take pity on Jerusalem, and implored them 'in God's name... to avenge the insult offered to our Lord'. The assembly's consent was vociferous: 'There was such an uproar and such a tumult that you might have thought the whole world was crumbling to pieces'. It is at this point that Villehardouin reveals that the goal of the expedition was Egypt, 'because from there the Turks could be more easily crushed than from any other part of their territory'. This was kept a close secret. But when the envoys left Venice, some of them making for Pisa and Genoa to solicit additional naval help, the foundations had been laid for a sea-borne expedition which could have completed the work of reconstruction started by the Third Crusade.

Before the problem of numbers could make itself felt the Crusade went through a crisis of leadership. On arriving back in Champagne Villehardouin found Count Thibaut ill, and his death soon afterwards deprived all the Crusaders from Champagne of their natural leader. Approaches to the Duke of Burgundy and the Count of Bar-le-Duc were rebuffed and at another general conference which took place at Soissons in June 1201 Villehardouin suggested that Boniface, Marquis of Montferrat, be offered the command not just of the Champagne Crusaders but of the entire army. As in the case of the Compiègne meeting, Villehardouin rather annoyingly mentions dissent without providing any details, before recording agreement to go ahead with the proposal. It was a natural choice. Boniface was famed as a commander and extremely well-connected. In the West he had kinship ties to both Philip II of France and Philip of Swabia, while in the East three of his brothers had married into the royal houses of Jerusalem and Byzantium. Boniface came to Soissons, accepted the offer and took the Cross. Overall the outcome of Thibaut's death was a strengthening of the Crusade.

No such ready solution presented itself in the summer of 1202 when the Crusaders gathered in Venice and it became apparent that they were far too few to meet the terms of the shipping contract. Villehardouin calculated that there were only about a third of the total needed, which implies about 12,000 Crusaders. For him the guilt lay with the many Crusaders who made their own way to the East, and he describes several such groups. Most importantly, a large proportion of the Flemish Crusaders travelled by sea, spending the winter of 1202–3 berthed at Marseilles. A group of French Crusaders also made their way southward to Marseilles and took ship there. Other French Crusaders crossed the Alps to Genoa, or travelled to Piacenza and then turned south to Apulia. Even Louis of Blois, whose own envoys had negotiated the contract alongside Villehardouin, was undecided which route to take and Villehardouin had to travel to Pavia to prevail on him to join the army at Venice. It is likely that in the course of the summer months of 1202 it became widely known that the army at Venice was facing severe financial difficulties and many recruits quite naturally preferred not to get involved. There was a danger that they would pay their passage money but never leave the lagoon. A broader issue of authority was also involved. The plenipotentiaries of 1201 had spoken only for the three magnates who sent them, not for the Crusaders en masse. The Pope had ratified their agreement with Venice, but it was largely on the basis of good-will that anybody not in the paid service of Boniface,

Baldwin or Louis came to embark at Venice. Even some who were subsidized by the leaders reneged on their obligations. Villehardouin referred to Gilles de Trasignies, a vassal of Baldwin who received 500 *livres* from the Count but embarked in Apulia. In his generous bequests to those who had taken the Cross with him, Thibaut of Champagne had specified that any beneficiary must swear on the Gospels to embark at Venice. Yet Villehardouin recorded that some of these people too broke their oaths.

After passage money had been collected from everybody who could pay, and the leaders had contributed their gold and silver table-ware, the Crusaders still lacked 34,000 marks. It might have proved possible to pay this within a year or so with the proceeds of Innocent III's tax on the Church, but in the meantime the army would have broken up. The Venetians, moreover, had prepared up to 500 vessels and they were ready for service now. What is sometimes portrayed as a golden opportunity for Venice to divert the Crusade actually spelled ruin for the city since its trade had been thoroughly disrupted and it had no other source of income. It is in this context of mutual desperation that what happened next should be viewed. This was a proposal from Venice that the debt should be postponed, to be repaid at a later date from plunder. In exchange, the Crusaders would help them to retake the Dalmatian port of Zadar (Zara) from the King of Hungary, who had taken it under his control after it rebelled against Venetian rule in 1180/81.

It is not easy to form a balanced view of the full implications of the Zadar proposal. Granted that it would be an attack on a Christian city, that city was (in Venetian eyes) guilty of rebellion. Taking Zadar need be no more of a diversion than, say, Richard I's sacking of Messina *en route* to the East during the Third Crusade. And after wintering there, the Crusaders could proceed to Egypt in the spring of 1203. On the other hand, since King Emeric of Hungary had taken the Cross, his lands (legitimately held or otherwise) had been taken under the protection of the Church. For the Crusaders to attack Zadar would be no better than their neighbours back home taking advantage of their absence to pillage their property. There were some that accepted this point but argued that the diversion was necessary in order to keep the army intact. Others felt that even this high aim could not justify the attack. Villehardouin, who had no time for this position, at this stage introduces a descriptive phrase which gives them scant justice, portraying them in a wholly negative light as 'those who wished the army to be disbanded'.

There was a further set of circumstances relating to the Crusaders' debate on the Zadar proposal which Villehardouin, somewhat disingenuously, only introduces once the decision has already been made to accept it. This was the presence in the West of a refugee Byzantine Prince, Alexius Angelus. One feature of Byzantium's complex malaise was chronic instability at the centre of power; since the death of Emperor Manuel Comnenus in 1180 Constantinople had suffered a series of palace revolutions. In the most recent coup, in 1195, Alexius's father Isaac II Angelus had been overthrown and blinded by his own brother Alexius III. Alexius Angelus came west seeking assistance to reinstate his imprisoned father, and in 1201–2 Alexius pressed his case with several of the people most closely involved in the organization of the Fourth Crusade. His most promising hope was Philip of Swabia, whose wife Irene was Alexius's sister. At Philip's court at Hagenau, at Christmas 1201, Alexius talked with Boniface of Montferrat, and from there he went to Rome where he had discussions with Innocent III in February 1202. The Venetians too knew of Alexius's arrival and travels.

This naturally furnishes a rich vein of speculation for historians in search of a conspiracy to explain the Crusade's diversion. The proposal that the Crusade should first make its way to Constantinople to reinstate Isaac, and then proceed southward to fight the Muslims with Byzantine help, was mooted at Hagenau and raised by both Alexius and Boniface at Rome. We do not know any details, but based on the terms which Alexius later offered to the Crusaders the proposal had its attractions. Innocent III disapproved of the idea and it was taken no further. This is as much as the evidence enables us to say. It has been suggested that the refusal of many Crusaders to make their way to the embarkation point at Venice was rooted in a wide-spread perception that a diversion to Constantinople had already been secretly planned. But there are perfectly sound explanations for their actions without resorting to the theory of conspiracy. As for the idea that the leadership offer made to Boniface of Montferrat, a leading vassal of Philip of Swabia, shows that the diversion was planned as early as the summer of 1201, this is a classic example of the selective use of circumstantial detail to support a predetermined explanation. On the other hand, it is perfectly legitimate to argue that an awareness of Alexius's offer being 'on the table' operated in favour of accepting the Zadar diversion, and that Zadar, in turn, was a stepping stone towards Constantinople. Not surprisingly, Alexius argued that his uncle's regime was unpopular and he predicted that the reinstatement of his father would be a speedy and straightforward process. The Venetian expectation that the remainder of the Crusaders' debt would be paid from booty, problematic if an assault was made on a 'hard' target like Egypt, became much less daunting if the Crusaders went first to a 'soft' one like Constantinople.

Villehardouin covers the debate over Zadar in just twenty words. In reality it was multi-faceted and heated. The scheme's opponents were angry and desperate men. In his account of the Crusade Gunther of Pairis echoed the views of his Abbot, Martin of Pairis:

> '...when our Martin saw not only the business of the Cross tied up in delays but also our entire army being forced to shed Christian blood, he did not know where to turn or what to do.'

Many looked for guidance to the papal legate, Peter Capuano. He shared the majority view that it was:

> '...more pardonable and less blameworthy to secure the greater good through means of the lesser evil, rather than to leave their Crusade vow unfulfilled and, retracing their steps homeward, to carry back with them infamy along with sin'.

Peter forbade Abbot Martin and other religious followers to abandon the Crusade; they were 'to stay with their comrades through every peril and to restrain them, insofar as it was possible, from shedding Christian blood'. The legate had other problems – the Venetians questioned his status and he had to travel to Rome to get it confirmed. This was undeniably convenient and the desire to avoid presiding over the attack on Zadar probably explains why Boniface of Montferrat too made his way to see the Pope at this point. There were many defections, and the effect on the Crusade's numerical strength was aggravated when the deserters met latecomers on the road and persuaded them to abandon the expedition or make their way to other ports. But if the remaining Crusaders were at best half-hearted, the Venetians were jubilant. The Crusade was moving in a direction which promised much and Dandolo himself took the Cross to accompany it. The Doge had the symbol of his vow sewn on the front of his cap of office to make it as conspicuous as possible. Many Venetians followed his example by taking the Cross. Villehardouin remarked that 'up to that day very few had done so', a remark almost as naïve as his comparison between the Doge's new-found enthusiasm for crusading and the negativity of those who were deserting the army.

The fleet sailed for Zadar in early October, arriving a month later. The dissenters now made a further attempt to prevent the attack, encouraged by the arrival of a letter from Innocent III forbidding an assault on any Christian city under pain of excommunication. This was an embarrassing development and it caused a number of Crusaders, ably represented by Guy, the Cistercian Abbot of Vaux-de-Cernay, to refuse to join in the siege, but the army as a whole was not deterred. On 24 November Zadar fell. As planned, the army and fleet wintered there. Boniface of Montferrat joined them and soon afterwards the leaders received a detailed proposal from Philip of Swabia on behalf of Alexius Angelus. The terms could hardly be more tempting. A lump sum of 200,000 marks would be handed over to the Crusaders and Venetians for division between them. Alexius would contribute a force of 10,000 Greeks to join the Crusade and he would maintain a body of 500 knights in Palestine for the rest of his life. He would provision the army for a full year, and he would compel the patriarch of Constantinople to restore the Orthodox Church to union with Rome.

When Alexius's father Isaac later learnt of these terms he was appalled by their generosity. Alexius almost certainly knew that he would never be able to meet them in full. So too did the Venetians, who were just as familiar with the debilitated resources of the Byzantine empire as the Greeks themselves. There was no need for a conspiracy on the part of Venice: all they had to do was to allow themselves to be carried along with the flow of events, and with Dandolo present to handle their interests, they would stand to benefit from the outcome. For many of the Crusaders, unaware for the most part of the empire's weakened financial condition, the proposals were highly attractive. They offered the prospect of the Crusade setting out for Egypt from Constantinople in the summer of 1203 massively reinforced, with ample provisions in hand and their debts to the Venetians fully paid. When stated thus, it was a strategic scenario that made sense – Villehardouin quotes supporters remarking that 'only by way of Egypt and Greece can we hope to recover the land oversea.' Crusaders of a chivalric inclination felt sympathy for the plight of Alexius Angelus and his blinded father. Others opposed the proposal vociferously on a variety of grounds. It was a further diversion, another attack on fellow-Christians, and it constituted outright disobedience to the wishes of Pope Innocent III. The Pope released the Crusaders (though not the Venetians) from the excommunication which they had incurred for attacking Zadar, accepting that necessity had driven them to it. But there was no reason to expect that he would show the same leniency twice.

The debate over Constantinople was as heated as that over Zadar. Villehardouin could not disguise the severity of the rift, though he insisted on portraying it in his usual biased terms: 'one party was continually working to break up the army and the other to keep it together.' Large-scale defections occurred during the winter of 1202–3. Even the legate Peter Capuano abandoned the Crusade, making his way to Palestine and rejoining the expedition only after it had sacked Constantinople. In April the fleet sailed from Zadar for Corfu. It was only here that the full extent of the opposition to Alexius's plan made itself felt – Villehardouin frankly admits that more than half the army resisted. In an emotional scene the Crusade's leaders begged the rebels not to bring about the army's disintegration. A compromise was reached. The stay at Constantinople was to be brief, and at any point after St Michael's Day (29 September), ships would be provided on demand for those who wanted to make their way separately to the Holy Land.

The fleet arrived before Constantinople in late June 1203. Even with the Venetian fleet present, the task before it would have been extremely difficult if Alexius III had mounted a resolute defence. Villehardouin comments that there was insufficient food for three weeks and that 'never, in any city, have so many been besieged by so few'. But the Crusaders experienced little difficulty in taking the all-important tower at Galata, across the Golden Horn from the city, on 6 July. This enabled the Venetians to break the great chain blocking the Golden Horn and to bring their ships into position to launch an attack on the weaker walls which ran alongside the Golden Horn. On 17 July the Venetians and Crusaders launched co-ordinated attacks on the sea wall and on the north-eastern stretch of Theodosius's impressive land walls. After gaining a large portion of the sea wall, the Venetians had to rush to the assistance of the Crusaders when Alexius III led a *sortie* against them. The end of the day saw a stand off, but during the night that followed Alexius panicked and abandoned the city. Isaac was released from captivity and his son crowned as Co-emperor.

In June Innocent III had written to veto the assault on Constantinople but his letter arrived too late to influence events. His reaction to the fall of the city was relatively benign, no doubt in part due to Alexius Angelus's promise that he would lead the Greeks back into union with Rome. Now crowned as Alexius IV, he found it impossible to keep his lavish promises to his allies. He played for time, proposing that he should hire the Venetian fleet for the year from September 1203 to September 1204, with the promise that he would release it to sail southwards in spring 1204. Once again discord broke out in the army, though less than at Corfu – it did after all make more sense to wait for spring than to leave Constantinople with autumn approaching. But relations between Latins and Greeks rapidly deteriorated. An anti-Latin riot on 19 August showed the depth of the resentment felt by the Greek population at the presence of the westerners. A few days later a fire begun by Latins spread to burn down much of the city. Alexius IV realized that it would be more in his interests to abandon his former allies. Villehardouin was a member of the armed delegation sent to the Blachernae Palace to present the Emperor with an ultimatum to meet the terms of his agreement with the Crusaders and Venetians. At a tense meeting it was scornfully rejected: as Villehardouin commented, 'thus the war began'.

The second conquest of Constantinople was an even more difficult prospect than the first had been. Winter set in, and food was in very short supply. The army consisted of no more than 20,000 men, too small a force to lay siege in the conventional sense to the biggest city in the Christian world. Most energy went into foraging to ensure bare survival. Moreover, the political situation which the Crusaders and Venetians confronted became more complex in January 1204 when Isaac II and Alexius IV were over-thrown and yet another Alexius, a great-great-grandson of Alexius I from the Ducas family, seized the imperial crown. It was essential that the allies should address the issue of what they would do with the city once they had captured it, and in March they drew up a partition pact. All plunder seized was to be pooled, and from it the Venetians were assured payment of the debt which the Crusaders still owed them. The empire itself was to be divided into quarters, one of which was set aside for an emperor who would be elected from amongst the Latins. The remaining three-quarters of the empire would be divided equally between Crusaders and Venetians. All the Crusaders would stay at Constantinople until March 1205 to assist the new regime, after which each man would be free to go or stay as he wished.

The assault in 1203 had revealed the comparative weakness of the sea wall running along the Golden Horn, so it was here that the attack was directed on 9 April 1204. The walls were so close to the sea that bridge-like structures fixed to the mast-heads of the Venetian vessels could be manoeuvred into position to gain access to its towers. Clumsy though they sound, these devices proved effective when used in conjunction with conventional scaling ladders, but the Greeks defended the towers well and the first attack was a total failure. Triumphantly the Greeks taunted the retreating Crusaders by letting down their pants and exposing their buttocks. But after making adjustments to their tactics the allies attacked again on 12 April and this time they succeeded in taking two towers. In a wonderful passage Robert of Cléry described how a small group, which included himself, his lord Pierre d'Amiens and his brother Aleaumes hacked their way through a bricked-up gateway at ground level. Aleaumes, who as a priest had no business to be fighting at all, was first through the gap though Robert admitted that he tried to hold his brother back by grabbing his foot as he crawled forward on hands and knees. Despite the personal intervention of Alexius V, Greek resistance to this adventurous group crumbled away and Pierre d'Amiens sent some sergeants to open up one of the gates. The Crusaders poured in. In their eyes the city was far from taken, for its size and population were so vast that they expected to have to fight for a month to come. They therefore camped with care near to the walls and towers they had taken. However, like Alexius III before him, Alexius V made good his escape from the city during the night. When the Crusaders awoke on 13 April there was no more fighting to be done.

Instead there was a great city to sack. The plundering of Constantinople lasted for three days and for the whole of the first day it was accompanied by another great fire, which had broken out during the night. This was not unusual in a city built largely of wood experiencing a power vacuum, as Moscow would discover in 1812. Villehardouin commented, without a hint of shame, that:

> '...this was the third fire there had been in Constantinople since
> the French and Venetians arrived in the land, and more houses
> had been burnt in that city than there are in any three of the
> greatest cities in the kingdom of France'.

The sack of Constantinople by the Crusaders and Venetians has been neither forgotten nor forgiven by the Greek world and those who admire its civilization. Sir Steven Runciman, a leading historian of the Crusades and a trained Byzantinist, believed that there was no greater crime in history. This was not because of the death toll involved, which was much less than in Jerusalem in July 1099. What was, and remains, shocking was the extent of the plundering and vandalism. Villehardouin paid it the tribute of a rare authorial intervention: 'Geoffrey de Villehardouin here declares that, to his knowledge, so much booty had never been gained in any city since the creation of the world'. In addition to precious metals and fabrics, jewellery, table ware, palace furnishings, arms and armour, some 10,000 horses were rounded up from the city's stud farms. Reaching for superlatives to convey the scale of what he had witnessed, Robert of Cléry wrote that the wealth of Constantinople had exceeded that of the forty next most important cities in the world combined.

The Crusaders and Venetians had anticipated this and before the assault an attempt had been made to lay down ground rules for acceptable behaviour.

Under pain of death, no woman should be raped or robbed of the clothes that she was wearing. No monk or priest should be assaulted and no church or monastery broken into. These rulings proved to be unenforceable. The pillaging was fuelled by drunkenness and accompanied by rape, casual brutality, and the senseless destruction of libraries and of *objets d'art* which were immovable. Nobles were tortured to make them reveal where they had hidden their most precious possessions. There was much sacrilege, caused in part by greed and in part by the wish to punish what was viewed as decades of schismatic practices. Nicetas Choniates, whose account of the sack seethes with indignation, left an unforgettable description of the ransacking of the city's most magnificent church, Santa Sophia, built by the Emperor Justinian in the sixth century. Its famous gold and silver furnishings and facings were torn down, hacked off and loaded onto pack animals while a camp follower ensconced on the patriarchal throne sang bawdy songs. Innocent III, who at first received news of the capture of the city with pleasure because Church union would now be achieved, was furious when he heard details of what had been inflicted on the city.

The pillaging of Constantinople forces us to consider the very nature of the Fourth Crusade, which to all intents and purposes came to an end after the success of the second siege. For some commentators on crusading, the ruthless sack of a Christian city speaks volumes about the true motivation of its perpetrators, while the Fourth Crusade, in turn, epitomizes all the crusading expeditions. If the experience of the Jews in 1096 and the Muslims in 1099 revealed the murderous bigotry of the Crusaders, that of the Greeks in 1204 demonstrated their insatiable greed. To assess the validity of such comments it is important to establish a profile of this expedition, above all to compare it with its predecessors. It is an approach which should also prove useful in dealing with the perennial problem of why the Crusade departed so thoroughly from its goal of regaining Jerusalem, although at heart (it must be said) that problem is insoluble.

There is nothing either in the origins or in the preaching of the Fourth Crusade, which would lead us to expect the motivation of its participants to be radically different from those of previous Crusaders. Although they intended from the start to go by sea, and embraced a strategy of attacking Egypt which meant that they might never see Palestine, the Crusaders continued to view themselves as pilgrims – *li pelerin* is the term constantly used by Villehardouin and Robert of Cléry to describe people who had taken the Cross. In his account of the Crusade Gunther of Pairis included a reconstruction of a sermon preached by Abbot Martin at Basle, and its main themes are wholly characteristic ones: the sanctity of the holy places, which were Christ's own patrimony; the devastating loss of the True Cross; the inspiring precedent of the First Crusade; and the indulgence to be earned by all who took the Cross. Villehardouin's emphasis is firmly on the attraction of the indulgence: 'many, on that account, were moved to take the Cross'. It is true that Abbot Martin goes on to talk about the expectation of material rewards: 'many from your ranks will acquire a greater prosperity even in material goods there than they will have remembered enjoying back here'. But too much should not be read into such comments – Gunther had an enormous admiration for Robert of Reims, and he is echoing Robert's account of Urban II's Clermont sermon. It would be wrong also to deduce anything from the largely secular tone of Villehardouin's history. He was a commander and a fighting man, not a monk. Other sources for the Crusade reveal devotional patterns broadly similar to those of the earlier expeditions.

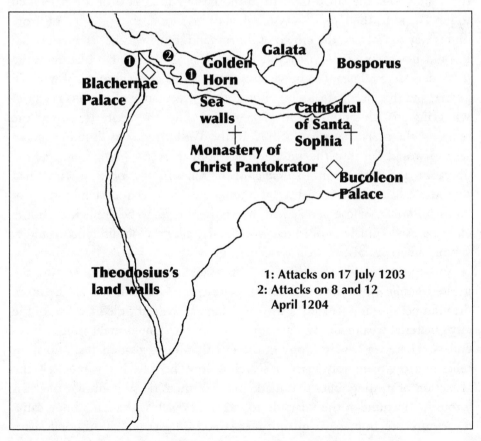

15. The Fourth Crusade at Constantinople.

In one respect the religious sensibilities of the Crusaders are highly conspicuous, while at the same time adding to their reputation for uncontrollable greed. This is their obsession with relics. There can be no doubt that a highly attractive feature of Alexius's appeal to the Crusaders to reinstate his deposed father was the chance it offered to visit Constantinople's relic collections. One of the issues on which Catholic and Orthodox piety converged was their mutual veneration of relics. Villehardouin may have exaggerated when he asserted that the city held half of all the relics in the world, but it is not hard to appreciate why he did so. In the interval between their first capture of Constantinople and their quarrel with Alexius IV, the Crusaders had ample opportunities to admire not just the city's material wealth, but also these religious riches. Robert of Cléry gives a vivid impression of the excitement and awe experienced by the rank and file on these occasions. The church of the Blessed Virgin of the Pharos, the main chapel of the Bucoleon Palace, held an astonishing array of relics from the crucifixion: two pieces of the True Cross, the lance-head from the Holy Lance, two of the nails used to pin Christ to the Cross, a crystal phial of his blood, the robe that he wore on his way to Calvary, the crown of thorns 'and so many other rich relics that I could not recount them to you or tell you all the truth'. Naturally the Crusaders were reluctant to move away from such a concentration of spiritual power, and this gave a strong impetus to their acceptance of Alexius's offer of wintering at Constantinople in 1203–4. For some the desire to possess the relics for themselves was irresistible. To the Western way of thinking such a seizure would fall into the category of 'pious thievery' (*furtum sacrum*), the liberation and 'translation' (*translatio*) of the relics from a location which had proved itself to be unworthy of them; and this was certainly true of Constantinople, whose people had shown themselves to be duplicitous in the extreme. Any saint who objected would, after all, have no difficulty in intervening supernaturally to stop it occurring.

Amongst other things, therefore, the sack of Constantinople was the greatest *furtum sacrum* in Christian history. To the Greeks it was all the more dreadful because it occurred at the same time as the unbridled looting of the city's material wealth and was accompanied by the same brutality and drunkenness. There was a grim irony in the fact that the Crusaders had sworn on relics not to violate holy space in search of loot, because it was precisely the attraction of stealing relics that made many of them do so. Gunther of Pairis wrote his account of the Crusade to explain how his Alsatian Abbey came to acquire the impressive quantity of sacred objects which Abbot Martin collected at Constantinople, and some aspects of the Abbot's behaviour were incongruous in the extreme, even after events had been carefully reshaped by Gunther. Accompanied by a chaplain, Martin headed for the church of the monastery of Christ Pantokrator and threatened to murder the custodian of the relics unless he handed them over. With the relics scooped up in their habits, the two men hurried back to the berthed ships. Others on their way to plunder asked Martin how he had got on: 'We have done well' was his beaming reply. He had indeed, for the full collection, reverently itemized by Gunther at the end of his account, amounted to more than fifty artefacts of wood, bone and stone. Overnight, through its Abbot's initiative, the Cistercian Abbey at Pairis acquired one of the greatest collections of relics in Western Europe.

As noted in the previous chapter, intention cannot necessarily be read from behaviour, and there is no call to deduce from these events that Martin of Pairis went on Crusade in order to acquire relics. We have already seen that he was alarmed by the diversion to Zadar and only remained with the army at the command of the papal legate. Driven by circumstances and trapped by events, Martin made the best use of the situation in which he found himself. The same was certainly true of many others in the army. April 1204 witnessed a disastrous convergence of circumstances: a city incomparably rich in both material and religious terms exposed to the attentions of an army of deeply-ingrained and brutal acquisitiveness. It should not be surprising to find this acquisitiveness present in 1204 because, as we saw in chapter one, it was a compelling feature of the society from which crusading sprang. In virtually all the crusading which had occurred since 1095 it had manifested itself in one guise or another. The habit of plundering was so embedded in the knightly mentality that an early apologist of the Knights Templar, the military-religious order established for the defence of the holy places in the early twelfth century, had to alert them to the devil's use of the anxiety aroused in their own mind by their pillaging in order to undermine their belief in their vocation. Nor were the Templars alone in their concern. Both Villehardouin and Robert of Cléry lamented the divisive effects of greed (*la covoitise del monde*, as Villehardouin put it) – Robert showed great bitterness at the 'bad faith and bad comradeship' shown by the barons, who robbed poor knights like himself of their fair share of booty at Constantinople. There was nothing inherently different between the behaviour of the Crusaders in 1204 and that of Richard I on Cyprus in 1191. The agreement made by the baronial plenipotentiaries and Venetians to divide all their conquests between them was an echo of an agreement reached by Richard I and Philip II before leaving on the Third Crusade. Even the partition pact of March 1204, whose

16. Coin of Richard I 1189–1199. Inadequate funding lay behind the crisis which the leaders of the Fourth Crusade faced at Venice in 1202.

cold precision has repelled historians and to some has seemed to be strong evidence of conspiracy, derived from the same habits. A medieval army besieging a great city needed an agreed programme for dealing with its hoped-for conquest just as much as it needed a plan of attack.

Without more convincing proof than we currently possess for the deliberate planning of diversion, we can read nothing into such circumstantial detail. All it tells us is that, for many different reasons, Constantinople, the 'queen of cities' (*regia civitas*), was a tremendously attractive destination for the Fourth Crusade. There is no reason to question Villehardouin's description of the astonishment felt by the Crusaders when they first saw the city: 'I can assure you that all those who had never seen Constantinople before gazed very intently at the city, having never imagined there could be so fine a place in all the world.' And a variety of factors relating to crusading at this stage in its development helped to promote the cause of diversion – notably the cost of travelling by sea, the inability of Innocent III to translate his personal wishes into workable mechanisms of control, and the evolution of a more sophisticated and flexible way of thinking about how Jerusalem might best be reconquered and retained. Against such a back-cloth, each stage in the Crusade's movement towards taking Constantinople in April 1204 can be explained as a rational response to a terrible predicament, a series of decisions made with the best of intentions, although collectively spelling doom for all Innocent III's hopes.

Having said that, it is possible to detect a certain change of tone, a slow slide and shift of expectations, as the Fourth Crusade progressed through the series of diversions which ended in the sack of Constantinople. To start with, one does not have to posit a radical divide between the way of thinking of Villehardouin's 'pilgrims' and that of the Venetians to suggest that the enthusiasm of the latter for the Crusade – once the Zadar diversion was agreed upon – tipped the balance in favour of the expedition's making its way to Constantinople. I have stressed that for the Venetians crusading could not be viewed separately from public policy and this was as true in 1201–4 as ever. It is not being cynical to see in Dandolo's assumption of the Cross an expectation that the Crusade's outcome was likely to be highly favourable to Venice. It was no light matter for the Doge to absent himself from the lagoon for a length of time which nobody could predict. Innocent III, for one, was concerned from the beginning about the consequences of Venetian involvement in the expedition. Then there is the actual constitution of the crusading host. On a number of occasions, at Venice, Zadar, Corfu and Constantinople, large groups of Crusaders had left, either to go home or to make their way separately to Palestine, rather than consent to a diversion or delay. Their reasons no doubt varied – not all were altruistic and it would be wrong to conclude that with their departure the army's collective conscience drained away. But those who remained were likely to be men who placed less of a premium on going to Palestine, who were more prepared to compromise, or whose habits of obedience were simply stronger.

From this point of view an incident which occurred as the fleet rounded the Peloponnese is revealing. It passed two ships bringing back home men who had earlier sailed to the East via Marseilles. Baldwin of Flanders sent over a skiff to make enquiries and a sergeant leapt into it and returned to join the army. Shouting up to his former companions on deck, he told them that they could keep his luggage: 'I'm going with these people, for it certainly seems to me they'll win some land for themselves'. Villehardouin saw this as a welcome conversion, but judging from the man's comment it seems more likely that he was making a shrewd assessment of how things were likely to go once the army reached Constantinople. Quite possibly the change of attitudes involved was too subtle and incremental for any single event to mark an abandonment of the Crusade's final objective. But if a single event had to be chosen, a good one would be the partition pact of March 1204. The Crusaders' final agreement with Alexius IV envisaged the departure of the fleet, with the Emperor's grateful assistance, in the spring of 1204. This was just about credible. In the partition pact, on the other hand, it was stipulated that everybody should remain for a full year after the capture of the city. It is doubtful that anybody could have seriously hoped that enough Crusaders would be prepared to resume their journey to the East at that point to make an expedition viable, or that ships would be available to carry them.

Terrible as it was, in one respect the sack of Constantinople differed radically from the capture of Jerusalem – the Crusaders did not massacre the Greeks in the name of religion. Their condemnation of Greek behaviour was unquestionably vigorous. Gunther of Pairis, venting the prejudice of a cloistered intellectual, and a snobbish and neurotic one at that, described the Greeks as morally degenerate: 'the mad race', 'a profane race', 'the scum of scum'. Constantinople was 'an evil city, full of deceit and unworthy of the sun's light', its population 'an idle, cowardly rabble... a people in whom evil deceit has found a comfortable home'. Villehardouin was more restrained but he did not conceal his belief that the Greeks were treacherous by nature. 'Judge for yourselves, after hearing of this treachery, whether people who could treat each other with such savage cruelty would be fit to hold lands or would deserve to lose them?' Given the Crusaders' own experience of the Greeks, it would have been odd if they had thought differently. Occasionally the language used went further, approaching the shrill rhetoric which had been voiced by the Bishop of Langres on the Second Crusade: Robert of Cléry wrote of the Greeks being condemned as 'the enemies of God' and 'worse than the Jews'. But there was no wholesale demonization. Indeed, the conquest of Constantinople both in 1203 and in 1204 was seen as a means of enforcing Church union, and this implied a sense of underlying fraternity. For Gunther of Pairis, the second capture of the city was a form of loving chastisement inflicted on erring fellow-Christians: 'remember they are brothers whom you overwhelm, who by their guilt have merited it for sometime.' Given the horrors that took place during the sack of Constantinople, such phrases leave a bad taste in the mouth. But they form one of several indications that, for all the brutality which they often used, the Crusaders were more than greedy thugs – their behaviour was accompanied by an awareness of moral considerations. It was a selective awareness, and at times it looks like camouflage rooted in practical needs, such as the fact that for those Crusaders planning to stay the Greeks would become subjects. But it was invariably present.

In the case of the Fourth Crusade, this moral sensibility emerges in two respects. The first was the handling of ethical issues on the expedition itself. Recording the death of Jean de Noyon, chancellor to Baldwin of Flanders, in the summer of 1204, Villehardouin commented that 'he was a very learned and saintly priest, whose eloquent preaching of the word of God had greatly comforted and sustained our troops'. There is plenty of evidence that the role of men like Jean de Noyon went beyond the pastoral.

When Innocent III manifestly failed to exert his will over the Crusade, such high-ranking churchmen stepped into the resulting vacuum. This applied above all to the heated debates about proposed diversions. In the contributions of the clerics on all these occasions we can see some of the first expressions of the more refined treatment of 'Just War', which the recent clarification of canon law by Gratian had made possible. The arguments which they put forward revolved around such key concepts as the recovery of lost property (Zadar), the reinstatement of the unjustly deposed (the first siege of Constantinople), vengeance for wrongs inflicted (the second siege), and the ending of schism (both sieges of Constantinople). We must presume that the senior clerics also assured the Crusaders that they could work alongside the Venetians, who should have been shunned by them since they had not been released from the excommunication imposed on them for attacking Zadar.

The clerics' role as the expedition's moral arbiters became most important in the winter and spring of 1203–4, when they informed the Crusaders that their second attack on Constantinople was justifiable and that it would not debar them from the Crusade indulgence. This was a matter of enormous concern to them. Up to this point their attacks on Christians had arisen from legal contracts, first with the Venetians and then with Alexius Angelus. With no contractual basis for this new assault, it was the more important that its moral rectitude be crystal clear. And Villehardouin's language was indeed clear:

> '"We therefore tell you", said the clergy, "that this war is just and lawful; and if you fight to conquer this land with the right intention of bringing it under the authority of Rome, all those of you who die after making confession shall benefit from the indulgence granted by the Pope". The barons and all the other Crusaders were greatly comforted and encouraged by this assurance.'

Nonetheless, military setback provoked a crisis of confidence. According to Robert of Cléry, the Crusaders were alarmed by the implications of their initial assault on Constantinople, 'they met together and were greatly troubled, and they said that it was for their sins that they were not able to succeed better at the city'. At this point the exhortations of Jean de Noyon, the Bishops of Halberstadt, Soissons and Troyes, and Abbot Simon of Loos, played a crucial role in rallying the dispirited men. 'The bishops and the clergy of the host consulted together and gave judgement that the battle was a righteous one and that they were right to attack them.' A return to God's favour was sought through the now-familiar exercise of expelling camp followers. It is remarkable that even at this advanced stage in the Crusade's diversion the Crusaders were troubled by their consciences. These required considerable massaging by the clerics in the army, who by now saw wonderful opportunities opening up for Church union, and quite possibly posts for themselves. The clerical triumphalism manifested in the southward march through Lebanon and Palestine in 1099 was thus replicated on the shores of the Bosporus.

The second respect in which the Crusade was subjected to moral criteria was retrospectively, in the way its chroniclers described it. Justifying diversion on the spot was one thing; interpreting it in terms of the history of the entire Crusade quite another. The jarring discrepancy between Innocent III's goals and the actual outcome of the Crusade could not be avoided. Villehardouin's response was similar to that of historians of the First and Second Crusades: like astonishing success and terrible failure, diversion from intended purpose was, above all, providential. It was another example of the inscrutable but unquestionable workings of God's will. For the Marshal, some events which occurred during the Crusade were so extraordinary that they could only be attributed to God. They included the storming of Zadar (notwithstanding the strength of its walls), the survival of the army intact despite the huge pressures which were exerted on it, Alexius III's abandonment of Constantinople and, above all, the capture of a city of 400,000 inhabitants by an army numbering some 20,000 Crusaders and Venetians. This celebration of the workings of providence was in complete harmony with the excitable tone of derring-do which Villehardouin used.

Gunther of Pairis also placed providence at the heart of his account of the Crusade.

> 'I do not believe that without the indisputable miracle of divine favour this exceedingly well-fortified city... could have been surrendered into the hands of a few, so suddenly, so openly, and so easily.'

His learning naturally enabled him to give the Crusade a more sophisticated treatment than Villehardouin, above all through his account's carefully fashioned structure. With his reverence for Robert of Reims, it was natural for Gunther to use Robert's history of the First Crusade as a model and to draw analogies throughout. In Gunther's account the conquest of Constantinople comes close to being as significant an event as the capture of Jerusalem. The great *furtum sacrum* of April 1204 naturally assisted this comparison – it has been pointed out that every event in the life of Christ which Abbot Martin mentioned in his Crusade sermon at Basle had a corresponding relic in the collection which Martin later stole. This formed an ingenious justification for the Crusade's diversion, but it carried with it the danger of drawing attention to the very tragedy which it was trying to disguise. Wonderful as they were, these relics were a constant reminder of the land that their 'liberators' were supposed to have returned to Christian hands.

The Fourth Crusade therefore acquired an ambivalent reputation. It was an astonishing military feat, worthy, its apologists claimed and contemporaries by and large accepted, of heroes like Achilles, Alexander and Charlemagne, but at the same time it constituted a massive diversion of effort and resources from the predicament of the Holy Land. Villehardouin and his fellow-Crusaders did not have the leisure to reflect on these issues in the spring of 1204. Almost exactly a half of the *CdC* deals with events which happened after the fall of Constantinople, between April 1204 and the death of Boniface of Montferrat in September 1207. They were years of relentless warfare as the conquerors strove to defend Constantinople and to extend their holdings. The election of a Latin emperor went smoothly enough. The candidates were Boniface of Montferrat and Baldwin of Flanders. The Crusaders were anxious to avoid a repetition of the bitter rivalry between Godfrey of Bouillon and Raymond of St Gilles over Jerusalem (the comparison with 1099 is interesting). They therefore agreed in advance that the unsuccessful candidate should be generously endowed with land so that he did not leave with all his supporters. Contrary to expectations it was Baldwin who won, and Boniface was granted Thessalonika. The actual partitioning of lands in accordance with the pact was carried out by twenty-four commissioners including, unsurprisingly, Villehardouin.

Much of this partitioning got no further than the parchment on which it was drawn up. At the heart of the problem lay the fact that the 'queen of cities' herself, the unrivalled attraction for conquerors, could not be held without a hinterland of some size in Thrace. The chief rival here was the Vlacho–Bulgar kingdom ruled by Kalojan (Ioannitsa). He was an ambitious man attracted by Latin culture: in 1199 he was recognized as king by Innocent III in exchange for his submission to papal authority. Shortly before the conquest of Constantinople Kalojan made overtures to the Crusaders but they were brusquely dismissed. As Robert of Cléry fully recognized, this arrogance was

a monumental blunder. At first its consequences were disguised by the continuing presence of the crusading host, which enabled the Franks to make some
impressive gains in 1204–5, including Adrianople and Philippopolis. But in
March 1205 the majority of the Crusaders left and the few fighting men who
remained were insufficient to create the conditions of security needed to
attract settlers from the West. Kalojan attacked and immediately stripped the
Latin empire of almost all its holdings outside Constantinople. Deprived of the
breathing space which had been crucial for the early settlers in Palestine and
Syria, the Franks were plunged into crisis. The Emperor Baldwin was
captured in April 1205 and died in prison. His brother Henry, who succeeded
him, had to face incessant attacks by both Kalojan and Theodore Lascaris, the
ruler of a Byzantine splinter-state at Nicaea. The last chapters of the *CdC*
graphically depict the new Emperor rushing from one front to another trying
to hold together a military situation which must have seemed hopeless.
Villehardouin made no bones about it:

> 'Geoffrey de Villehardouin, Marshal of Romania and Champagne,
> and author of this chronicle, has no hesitation in affirming that no
> people, at any moment in their history, had to bear such a heavy
> burden of war.'

As it transpired, the Latin empire survived for another half a century. The
main reason was not any substantial accumulation of land or resources but a
slackening of external pressure following Kalojan's death in 1207. This gave
Henry the chance he needed to stabilize his frontiers both in Europe and in
Asia. His death at the age of just forty in 1216 robbed the empire of its finest
ruler, though it is very doubtful whether even Henry would have proved as
successful a state-builder as he was a fire-fighter. The empire was an alien
import with no indigenous support. It came to depend for its survival on
Venetian assistance, the ruthless exploitation of Constantinople's remaining
wealth, and the divisions between the various Greek regimes in exile, which
delayed any attempt to reconquer the city. Venetian help dwindled from the
1230s, by which time it was obvious that the horse they were backing was a
non-starter. Constantinople's wealth, including its store of relics, was not
limitless and by the 1250s the lead from the palace roof was being stripped
to raise cash. In July 1261, when the city's garrison was away taking part in
an expedition in the Black Sea, a force sent by Michael Palaeologus from the
Byzantine state at Nicaea used the opportunity to seize Constantinople.
Typically, this news made scarcely any impression in the West.

Villehardouin's downbeat ending was not, therefore, an inappropriate commentary on the empire which he had done so much to create. Nonetheless, the Fourth Crusade did give rise to one strong principality in Greece. In February 1205 Boniface of Montferrat, encamped at Nauplion in the northern Peloponnese, received an audacious proposal from Villehardouin's nephew. He was also called Geoffrey, and he suggested that he and a companion called William de Champlitte should be provided with a band of knights to conquer the rest of the peninsula. Villehardouin clothed his nephew's proposal in classic *conquistador* language; prosperous land lay ready for the taking, all that was needed was a vigorous show of strength. With a force numbering just 500 men, these two military entrepreneurs succeeded in subjugating most of the Peloponnese (Morea). The principality of Achaea, as it was called, achieved the viability which eluded the Latin empire. Immigration from France made possible the creation of a stratified aristocracy of fief-holders, into which some members of the indigenous Greek nobility were integrated. Numerous castles were constructed to give visible expression to their new lordships. Strong trading links with Italy were built up. The court of the Villehardouin princes, especially that of Geoffrey II (1228–46) achieved a certain renown in Western Europe as a centre of chivalry. In 1224 Pope Honorius III called the states established in the wake of the Fourth Crusade *nova Francia*, and in the Peloponnese this ambitious vision was at least partially realized.

The outcome of the summons to Crusade which Innocent III issued in August 1198 was a dramatic change in the configuration of forces in the eastern Mediterranean. It affected the entire region from the Black Sea in the north to Crete (acquired by Venice) in the south. The effect on crusading too was bound to be considerable. The 'official' end of the Fourth Crusade is notoriously hard to pin down. It has been pointed out that Innocent III continued to refer to the conquerors of Constantinople as 'pilgrims' or 'Crusaders' for three years after the city's fall in 1204, exhorting the baronial leadership to fulfil their vows to liberate the Holy Land. In the light of the critical situation which was developing at Constantinople this was bizarre, but it reflected part of the justification of conquest which apologists like Villehardouin were working into shape at the time. In fact the 'stepping stone' idea proved remarkably resilient, though it is not easy to disentangle genuine hopes, *ex post facto* rationalizations concocted by men like Gunther of Pairis, and pipe-dreams. In 1205 the Provençal troubadour Raimbaut de Vaqueiras, who came on Crusade with Boniface of Montferrat, rhapsodized that 'by us will Damascus be assaulted, and Jerusalem conquered, and the kingdom of Syria liberated for the Turks find this in their prophecies'. It is too easy to dismiss such comments as camp-fire consolation: high aspiration, especially when linked in this way to prophecy, formed a crucial element of crusading's appeal.

Military reality, however, dictated that the maintenance of the hard-pressed Latin establishment in Romania, as this whole region came to be called, should itself be viewed in crusading terms, and the region's defence was added to the growing list of causes for which crusading indulgences and privileges were offered. There was a seamless transition from the Fourth Crusade itself, for the papal legate Peter Capuano attempted to staunch the mass haemorrhage of Crusaders that took place in April 1205 by offering the full Crusade indulgence in exchange for a further year's service. Peter went in person to the ships where the Crusaders had already embarked and begged them in tears 'to have pity on their fellow-Christians, as also on their lords who had died in battle, and remain there for the love of God'. In June 1206 another legate, Cardinal Benedict of Santa Susanna, guaranteed the Crusade indulgence to any of the soldiers of the Regent Henry who should fall in battle. It was not long before the popes followed their legates' lead by issuing Crusade bulls specifically for Romania. They acted partly through conviction (there was, after all, now a Latin patriarch at Constantinople, albeit with painfully little to do), and partly in response to the desperate pleas which arrived from Romania, coupled with strenuous lobbying from the settlers' families and patrons in the West. The first such Crusade was preached on behalf of Thessalonika in 1223, and others followed for the Latin empire and the principality of Achaea.

The Crusaders to whom Peter Capuano made his tearful appeal in April 1205 were not won over. Their situation was, of course, exceptional for they had been on campaign for two and a half years and having made the decision not to settle were probably desperate to see their families again; but their negative response became characteristic when the full apparatus of preaching was deployed in localities in the West. Only when family interests were directly involved did many people take the Cross, as in the Crusade preached for Thessalonika. It was striking that when Pope Gregory IX made a forceful attempt in 1236 to switch ('commute') the vows of a large group of French Crusaders who had taken the Cross for the Holy Land, so that they would go instead to help Constantinople, he was ignored. Crusaders had an autonomy which they were not prepared to see eroded. To some extent this diluted the threat that the rival needs of Romania posed to the Holy Land but there was still a negative balance sheet taking into account the diversion

17. Thirteenth-century knight in plate armour.

of Crusade funds, over which the popes had much more control, and of course the attention of the popes and their direction of Crusade preachers.

More importantly, there was the condition of Graeco–Latin relations after 1204. The impact of the sack and occupation of Constantinople was catastrophic, making its impression felt right up to the city's fall to the Ottoman Turks in 1453. It was not until the early fourteenth century that the major courts of the West, including the papacy, reconciled themselves to the restored Byzantine empire. Even when a thaw did occur any movement towards joint military operations was hindered by mutual suspicion whose roots lay in memory of the events of 1204. There were too many Greeks who agreed with the famous remark attributed to Lucas Notaras, chief minister to the Emperor Constantine XI, that the sultan's turban was preferable to the cardinal's hat. It is possible to attribute too much to the Fourth Crusade. Byzantine-Crusader co-operation was from the very beginning imperilled by misunderstandings and by the basic strategic consideration that Jerusalem lay outside Byzantium's sphere of interest. By the time of the Fourth Crusade the Byzantine empire was also suffering from such deep weaknesses that its military capability was much diminished. Yet the empire was remarkably resilient, it had overcome terrible crises in the past and would experience an impressive revival under the Palaeologan dynasty after 1261. In the fourteenth century, moreover, the strategic situation in the East shifted fundamentally, bringing the interests of Latins and Greeks much closer together. Military co-operation between them became easier to implement if goodwill and trust had been evident, which they were not. Taking the broadest perspective, the Crusades in the Mediterranean world were conflicts between the Christian and Islamic religions, and the former included the Orthodox Greeks. We have seen that the Crusaders regarded them as brothers who had gone astray. They must be brought back into the sheep-fold through loving chastisement, the price of their sinful behaviour being the forfeiture of their wealth, land and relics. It is not surprising that the Greeks saw things differently. In 1204 fraternity itself was almost destroyed, and the cost to both Greeks and Latins was extraordinarily high.

3

JOINVILLE AND THE 'VIE DE SAINT LOUIS':

CRUSADING AND PIETY

Most tourists in Paris pay a visit to Nôtre Dame. Far fewer undertake the short walk needed to see the Sainte-Chapelle, the smaller but no less exquisite masterpiece of Gothic architecture tucked away in the courtyard of the nearby Palais de Justice. Just 110 ft long and 55 ft wide, the two-storey Sainte-Chapelle was built by King Louis IX of France between 1242 and 1247 to house the relics, which he was in the process of buying from the impecunious Emperor of Constantinople, Baldwin II. The most important relic in a collection generally centred on the events of Christ's Passion was the Crown of thorns. The chapel was dedicated on 25 or 26 April 1248, in the presence of the King and the papal legate who was preaching the Crusade. Just a few weeks later the King went to Nôtre Dame to receive the pilgrim insignia, which announced his imminent departure on Crusade. Thereafter the chapel became associated with the crusading aspirations of Louis and his successors on the French throne. A legend developed that Louis himself brought back the chapel's relics from his first Crusade. When the King had his fragment of the True Cross brought down from its raised reliquary in the chapel in March 1267, a member of his council who was watching predicted that he was about to take the Cross for a second time; he was right. In October 1332 it was in the Sainte-Chapelle that Louis's great-grandson, King Philip VI, announced his plan 'to cross the sea to assist in the conquest of the Holy Land'. The setting was an assembly of France's nobles and senior clerics, and they were asked to swear on Louis's collection of relics that they would respect the succession should Philip die while overseas. The chapel had become a shrine not just for its relics but for France's crusading conscience.

The chief glory of the Sainte-Chapelle is its stained glass, about two-thirds of it original. Beginning with the Creation, it recounts events in sacred history through the Old Testament and the life of Jesus to the consecration of the chapel itself. The glass forms a telling and moving reminder of the devotion of St Louis for the Holy Land. As he lay dying he sighed the words 'O Jerusalem, O Jerusalem!' It was the King's dedication to the desperate needs of the Holy Land that took him on his two Crusades and caused him to give them as impressive a form as possible. The organization of these ventures placed a crucial stamp on his reign, and the memory of them shaped the actions and thinking of French kings in the late Middle Ages. Louis's obsession with crusading was not unparalleled in his generation; what was unique was his ability to use on behalf of crusading the resources and reputation of a monarchy which was going through its most successful period of growth and achievement. Between 1244, when he took the Cross for the first time, and 1270, when he died on Crusade in Tunisia, Louis IX dominated crusading and he was the chief hope of the increasingly frail Frankish establishment in Palestine and Syria. His canonization in 1297 occurred because of the sanctity of his personal life and the miracles that he performed, but it is undeniable that his commitment to crusading also played a strong part. In the history of the Crusades Louis occupies a very special place.

We encounter Louis through Jean de Joinville, holder of the hereditary seneschalship of Champagne, who between 1305 and 1309 wrote a life of the saint, (*Vie de saint Louis*, hereafter *VdsL*). Joinville was born in 1224/5, a decade later than his subject. He died on Christmas Eve 1317. Unlike his fellow-Champenois Villehardouin, Joinville tells us exactly why he wrote his text. He dedicated his book to Louis, King of Navarre and Count of Champagne, and wrote that the Queen of France, Louis's mother Joan of Navarre, 'begged me most earnestly to have a book written for her containing the pious sayings and the good deeds of our King, Saint Louis'.

Joan died in April 1305 and on completing his 'life', Joinville sent it to her son, heir to her possessions and titles in Champagne, in the hope that Louis and his brothers, the sons of King Philip the Fair and Joan, 'may take some good examples from it, and put them into practice, thus winning themselves favour in the sight of God'.

As a composition, the *VdsL* is *sui generis*. It has some of the attributes of a conventional saint's life, especially in the opening section, which consists of anecdotes pulled out of the main text and brought together to demonstrate Louis's devout behaviour. Joinville's veneration of his canonized friend is crystal clear: he built an altar for St Louis in his chapel of St Lawrence at Joinville, endowed Masses for it, and at the time of completing the *VdsL* was lobbying with Louis of Navarre for some of the saint's relics to place there. The hagiography, however, never becomes oppressive and there is little danger of its impairing the value of Joinville's recollections – in fact the problems posed by hindsight and simple forgetfulness are probably greater. Joinville presents a balanced picture of Louis, which includes some pointed criticisms of his friend. He complains about the way Louis handled the booty won at an early stage in his first Crusade, and he shakes his head over the King's lack of interest in his wife and children. 'In my opinion it does not seem right and proper for a man to be so detached from his own family.' This is not the language of a slavish admirer.

Joinville hoped that his recollections of events that had happened half a century earlier would influence the behaviour of the royal family and this didactic intent also had some impact on his text. As a very old man he had little to lose, and did not pull his punches about his opinion that Philip the Fair's administration had departed far too much from the excellent example set by Louis IX. 'Let the King who now reigns over us turn from doing wrong, and in such a way that God will not smite him cruelly, either in himself or in his possessions.' But as in the case of Joinville's treatment of Louis's personality, a sense of balance prevails. Denigration of Philip the Fair's officials did not cause Joinville to exaggerate the successes of Louis IX's government, however great his respect for the King's intentions. Above all, Louis's Crusades had proved to be failures, and Joinville makes no attempt to disguise that fact or to gloss over the suffering and privations which failure brought with it. In fact his descriptions of what the captured French endured are minor classics of prison literature. He admits that mistakes were made and he follows the line established in the aftermath of the Second Crusade in attributing failure to wicked behaviour which alienated God from the Crusaders' cause.

Joinville's text is, then, to some extent hagiographic and didactic – much more importantly, though, it is a set of personal memoirs and a portrayal of a deep friendship. Even more than Villehardouin, Joinville has the ability to communicate a powerful sense of immediacy. It was presumably this ability, coupled with Joinville's age and the astonishing strength of his memory, which led the Queen to commission his book. It springs from his intense interest in human affairs in all their forms, but particularly when they are unusual or fantastic. He cannot resist giving descriptions of the way of life of the Bedouin and the Cumans (Kipchak Turks), the behaviour of the Old Man of the Mountain, the Lord of the Assassins who wielded authority over Shi'i Muslims from his castles in northern Iran, and the rise of the Mongols; they were not essential for his narrative purpose but he assumed that his readers would share his fascination. He had a strong interest in clothing which caused him time and again to record what he and the King were wearing: more than sixty years after his first meeting with Louis, at Saumur in 1241, he claimed that he could remember exactly how the King was dressed. Few medieval writers rival Joinville in their command of visual and aural detail. The cramped conditions and perils of life on board ship, the chaos and clamour of hand-to-hand combat, and the easy comradeship of the camp, are described with magical effect.

In one unforgettable passage Joinville described how the youthful Count of Eu disrupted his meals when the two were neighbours in the Crusaders' camp near Sidon.

> 'The Count, who was a very ingenious fellow, had rigged up a miniature ballistic machine with which he could throw stones into my tent. He would watch us as we were having our meal, adjust his machine to suit the length of our table, and then let fly at us, breaking our pots and glasses.'

This mastery of the anecdote naturally paid dividends when it came to portraying his own friendship with the King. For it is through story after story that Joinville slowly creates a convincing picture of Louis's piety, charity, humility and innate sense of fair play, of his patient endurance of misfortune and his absolute reliance on God and the saints. The friendship of the two men was solidly rooted in their shared veneration for the Holy Land. Joinville was one of the few who advised that Louis should remain in the East after his release from captivity in Egypt; we might be tempted to question this were it not for the fact that Joinville bolstered his advice with the critical comment

pres henry le secunt regna Richard sun fiz. x. aunz̄e
temp̄ si entre paȳant de la t̄ere seȳnt fuit pis œl duk̄
de Ostriz par eyde del Roy Phylippe de fraunce. e fuit reyn̄t hors
de pison pur cent mil lyueres de argent. e pur œl rauncun fu
tent les Chaliz de Engletere pus. des Eglȳses e vendūz. puis
fuit tret de vn quarel de Alblast al Chastel de Chalezun. d̄t
tte vers si fet: Xp̄e tui calicis: predo fir preda calicis.

18. Imprisonment of Richard I, representing the King's imprisonment by the
Duke of Austria on his way home from the Holy Land.
From a thirteenth-century series of illuminations of English kings from
Edward the Confessor to Edward I.

that so far the King had not spent much of his own money, so he could afford to stay longer. The incident is revealing. It shows Joinville unafraid to speak his mind to the King, a quality which Louis firmly respected, and it is followed by a classic Joinvillean moment. Joinville stood at the window, with his arms through the bars (a fine example of the small details which set Joinville apart as storyteller) reflecting wistfully on what had happened. Louis came up to him and cupped his hands over Joinville's head. Not knowing whom it was Joinville snapped irritably. Louis did not take offence, but instead thanked him for his advice, which he subsequently followed.

To some commentators this story seems ingenuous, to others contrived; and it has to be admitted that there was probably nobody alive in 1309 who could challenge its veracity. What matters is that it reflects an intimacy, trust and mutual respect between King and seneschal, which cannot seriously be questioned. In addition to their devotion to the Holy Land, the two men shared a sense of humour and a natural sociability. Their friendship was strong enough for Joinville to record rebukes and points of difference. During the voyage back to France Joinville was placed in charge of safety in the King's galley, and one night there was a serious fire in the Queen's cabin. Next day Joinville kept his head down, hoping it would pass over, but the King told members of his household what had happened. Turning to Joinville, he gave him strict instructions to ensure that all fires except the main fire in the hold were extinguished, before going to bed at night. 'And take note that I shall not go to bed either till you come back to tell me this has been done.' For his part, Joinville knew that given the King's exceptional honesty, there were some things which it was better for him not to know. So when Philippe de Nemours made the mistake of telling Louis that the ransom paid for his release from Muslim captivity was actually 10,000 *livres* short, Joinville stamped on his foot to make him shut up.

This abundance of colour and anecdote, focused on the close rapport between the biographer and his subject, makes Joinville's text a particularly fine source for reconstructing the ideas and attitudes of crusading enthusiasts in his age. It is likely that Joinville was unusual in his ability to give full expression to his piety. At Acre in 1250–1, aged just twenty-six, he wrote a sophisticated commentary on the Apostolic Creed; on the other hand every medieval generation produced a number of devout and literate laymen of this type. And the *VdsL* is not an isolated document, which defies critical control. Joinville fitted a general trend to the extent that members of the laity were by this time making their views on crusading increasingly clear. For example, we have a range of opinions about crusading expressed in vernacular verse of beauty and power by Rutebeuf, a contemporary of Joinville and another enthusiastic advocate for the Holy Land. It was a development to which Joinville's homeland of Champagne made particularly strong contributions. To a much greater extent than in the case of the early Crusades, we enjoy direct access to the ways of thinking of Crusaders from the ranks of the lay aristocracy, instead of approaching them through the writings of clerics.

No contemporary of Louis IX and Joinville could fail to be aware of the desperate condition of the Holy Land. The essential problem faced by the Franks was similar to that of the Crusaders who stayed at Constantinople in 1204: the group of ports that had been recaptured with such effort by the Third Crusade possessed insufficient hinterland. The Franks had lost too much territory and too many castles. They were unable to reconstruct the defensive perimeter ingeniously put in place in the twelfth century or to regain the strategic initiative which they had held for much of the time up to the rise of Saladin. With the benefit of hindsight we can see that despite this they had very solid advantages. Italian control of the sea-ways meant that assistance could reach them from the West without fear of hindrance from the Muslims, while the trade routes which helped sustain the interest of the Genoese, Pisans and Venetians brought in customs revenues so substantial that they made Acre into one of the richest ports in the entire Mediterranean. On land there was a counterpart to the naval support provided by the Italians, in the form of the troops fielded by the Military Orders, the Templars, Hospitallers and Teutonic Knights. Most importantly, the vast empire won by Saladin fragmented under his successors, the Ayyubids. Family quarrels not only prevented any unified drive on the part of the Ayyubid Sultans to push the Franks into the sea for good, but also offered opportunities for alliances cutting across religious boundaries. Very little of this, however, was apparent at the time. The impression given was one of exceptional vulnerability – a few towns held by the Franks, inhabited by embattled élites with stretched nerves living in fear of a great Muslim offensive. From about 1240, moreover, the countryside between these towns became unsafe due to the arrival of bands of Khwarismian Turks, displaced from their homeland by the Mongols and living as brigands. Joinville describes how by 1253 even the coastal road from Sidon to Tyre had become highly dangerous. The situation of the resident Franks came to resemble that of European planters in Malaysia or Indochina after 1945, conducting a grim daily battle against Communist insurgency while expecting expulsion by the Nationalists as soon as the latter managed to overcome their internal disputes. Again Joinville communicates well the prevailing atmosphere of crisis: on being told by Louis IX in 1254 that they were setting sail from Acre on his birthday, 25 April, he remarked that the King 'might in future say that on that day he had been reborn, for certainly he had entered on a new life when he escaped from that perilous land'.

These perils were constantly expounded to the Catholic world by Crusade bulls issued by the papal court, and they were alluded to in the liturgical prayers on behalf of the Holy Land which were offered up on a regular basis in all cathedrals, churches and chapels. The result was intense concern that all the gains made by the First Crusade might be swept away and any chance of regaining Jerusalem itself lost forever. Devotion to the Holy Land was as strong as ever, it was in complete harmony with the desire to associate with Christ's life and sufferings, which the Franciscans encouraged. But what is most striking about the period between the end of the Fourth Crusade in 1204 and Louis's first assumption of the Cross forty years later is the inability of Christendom's religious and political authorities to channel this concern and devotion into effective action. Between 1212 and 1229 no fewer than three Crusades demonstrated, in different but equally telling ways, the yawning gulf which had opened up between crusading zeal and military achievement. The first was the 'Children's Crusade' of 1212. The name itself is a misnomer, since the 'children' (*pueri*) were largely adolescents and young people from northern France and the Rhineland. They seem to have taken the Cross without reference to any attempts to organize leaders, supplies or (crucially, given the shift in strategic thought which had taken place) shipping to take them to the East. Inevitably the movement ended in disillusionment and fraud, but it was followed by a series of such 'popular Crusades'; one such, the *Pastoureaux* or 'Shepherds' Crusade', broke out in France in 1251 when news circulated of the King's defeat and imprisonment in Egypt.

As far as we can tell from sources which are for the most part hostile, participants in the 'Children's Crusade' and the *Pastoureaux* were motivated by devotion reminiscent of that which had characterized the initial wave of the First Crusade. They were obsessed with regaining Jerusalem and the True Cross, they were strongly influenced by apocalyptic programmes and they were extremely hostile to the Jews. Although impossible to control and thus ultimately fruitless, their enthusiasm was in itself encouraging, and it is possible that the 'Children's Crusade' was one factor which led Pope Innocent III in 1213 to set in motion the Fifth Crusade, with the goal of recovering Jerusalem. Between 1217 and 1221 successive contingents of Crusaders sailed to the East, in spring and autumn voyages (*passagia*). At no other time were the benefits of Christian control over the Mediterranean Sea

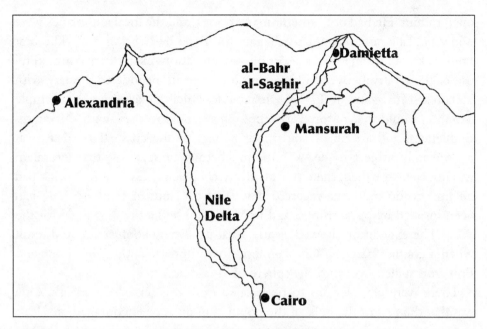

19. St Louis's Crusade in Egypt.

more clearly shown. Some of the arriving Crusaders fought in Palestine, but the majority took part in a prolonged attempt, lasting from 1218 to 1221, to implement the strategy of securing Jerusalem through an assault on Egypt. That objective was very nearly achieved – the Crusaders took the port of Damietta in 1219 and the Egyptian Sultan al-Kamil made an offer to hand back all the lands west of the Jordan, including Jerusalem, in exchange for the Crusaders' withdrawal. But thanks to miscalculations and divisions amongst the Crusade's leaders, the Sultan's offer was rejected. A southward advance along the Damietta branch of the Nile ended in defeat and the evacuation of the army with nothing to show for its efforts.

One reason for the failure of the Fifth Crusade was the prevarications of the Holy Roman Emperor, Frederick Barbarossa's grandson Frederick II. He had taken the Cross in 1215, and when he was crowned as Emperor in 1220 he promised Pope Honorius III that he would sail to the assistance of the Crusaders fighting in Egypt. It is likely that Frederick's arrival would have given the Crusade the leadership which it desperately needed, and his continuing failure to fulfil his vow played a major part in poisoning papal-imperial relations after the collapse of the Fifth Crusade. In 1227 Frederick set out from Brindisi, but he fell ill at sea and put into Otranto. Pope Gregory IX was so exasperated that he excommunicated Frederick, and when the Emperor finally reached Acre in September 1228, there were few options open to him. He had not brought many troops, and the local authorities were understandably anxious not to alienate the Pope by assisting him. The best Frederick could achieve was a sort of public relations exercise: making skilful use of the rivalry between Damascus and Cairo he negotiated a treaty with Sultan al-Mu'azzam of Egypt whereby Jerusalem (excluding the Temple Mount) would be restored to the Christians together with Nazareth, Bethlehem, and a strip of land joining them to the coast. The treaty was immediately subject to heavy criticism: because it specified that Jerusalem was not to be fortified, the city was effectively defenceless. But Frederick had no time to do more; he received news that his lands in southern Italy had been invaded by papal troops, and in May 1229 he hastily embarked for the West. The expedition showed clearly what paralyzing confusion could result when a conflict between Christendom's two supreme authorities, Pope and Emperor, spilled over into the sphere of crusading.

There were clear lessons to be learned from this series of setbacks. One was that the zeal of the bulk of the population must be encouraged, not least so as to secure their intercessionary prayers, but without returning to the age of the armed pilgrimage. The second was that control over a Crusade must be both concentrated and sustained, in terms of its organization, direction and command in the field. And the third was that it was essential to act in harmony with the Pope and more broadly with the Church. In preparing for the Fourth Crusade Innocent III had laid down the principle that the Church should shoulder much of the expense of crusading, but it was only possible to implement this if good-will and trust prevailed. St Louis was fortunate – the prosperous condition of his kingdom, the unquestioned prestige that the French monarchy enjoyed, and the healthy state of his relations with Pope and Church, all favoured the application of these lessons. It remains true that crusading was, as one historian has put it, a 'challenge' for Louis. It was challenging because it entailed maximizing the authority and resources which the French Crown had built up, to achieve the *efficacia* which Innocent III had emphasized but failed to realize on either of the great Crusades to the East that he had launched. In a broader perspective, Louis was undoubtedly aware that no Crusade to the East since the First Crusade had achieved its goals.

Following the logic of that last sentence, one is tempted to ask why Louis IX threw himself with energy and conviction into an enterprise which had accumulated such a forbidding track record of defeats and stalemates. Just such a question was posed of the King himself during his captivity by the amir Husam al-Din:

'How did your majesty, given all the virtue and good sense
which I observe in you, conceive the idea of boarding a ship and
riding the waves to come to a country populated by Muslims
and warriors, with the idea of conquering it and making yourself
its lord?'

Unfortunately Louis's only reply was to smile. The answer that the Victorians
would have given to Husam al-Din's question, that Louis and his contemporaries lived in an Age of Faith, is not in fact wide of the mark, provided that
it is properly contextualized. In the mid-thirteenth century the practice of
crusading was thoroughly embedded within the consciousness of Catholics –
it reached outward from the individual's religious experience in Church,
through family, region and nation, to a conception of a Christian 'people'
which had superseded the Jews in God's affection. It is most clearly visible as
a thread running through the history of noble families, a development of
which St Louis and Joinville represent excellent examples. In the King's case
two threads entwined: on his father's side there had been a Crusader in almost
every generation since the First Crusade, while his maternal grandfather
Ferdinand of Castile had won the greatest victory of the *Reconquista* at Las
Navas de Tolosa (1212). As for Joinville, his crusading inheritance was rich
even for a nobleman born in one of France's crusading heartlands. His great-
grandfather Geoffrey III had accompanied Henry of Champagne to the Holy
Land in 1147. His grandfather Geoffrey IV had fought and died at Acre on
the Third Crusade. One uncle, Geoffrey V, had gone to Acre with Geoffrey
IV, and, together with his brother Robert, had taken the Cross again for the
Fourth Crusade. Joinville's father Simon had taken the Cross to fight the
Cathar heretics in the Albigensian Crusade and had gone on to serve in the
Fifth Crusade.

Joinville was well aware of his ancestors' deeds, when he was in Syria he
retrieved the shield of Geoffrey IV and brought it back to the chapel of St
Lawrence at Joinville, where he installed it together with a commemorative
tablet. The *VdsL* also provides a textbook example of relatives clubbing
together to defray the expenses of crusading, for Joinville joined forces with
two cousins who had also taken the Cross, to hire a ship at Marseilles. Joinville
was intensely proud of his lineage and never missed a chance to celebrate his
many and far-flung kinsmen. This was particularly true of the Count of Jaffa,
whose mighty galley at Damietta is described in terms which bring it roaring
to life: 'what with the flapping of the pennons, the booming of the drums,
and the screech of Saracen horns on board, you would have thought a thun-

derbolt was falling from the skies'. Other important relatives also make brief appearances. When he was captured, and an amir asked if he was related to the Emperor Frederick II, Joinville replied that 'I had reason to believe that my lady mother was his first cousin'. At Acre, when he thought that Louis would return to France leaving him in the Holy Land, he considered serving Bohemond V, Prince of Antioch, 'who was a relative of mine, and had already asked me to come and join him'. And on his return to France he paid a call as soon as he could on 'my niece the Dauphine of Vienne, my uncle the Count of Chalon, and the Count of Burgundy, his son'.

It is understandable that men like Joinville should view their personal engagement in crusading at least partly in terms of family legacy and dynastic honour, when one recalls how families had borne the heavy cost of participation ever since the First Crusade. It helps make sense too of the remarkable legal ruling that unfulfilled crusading vows were subject to inheritance, alongside other debts of the deceased. This ruling was typical of many which were applied as canon lawyers turned their attention to crusading. There were good reasons for them to do so. In the first place, it was in the early thirteenth century that crusading became fully distinguishable from pilgrimage as a devotional practice; more than anything else this was due to Pope Innocent III's description of the Crusader's indulgence as a reward for service which was bestowed by the Church, as opposed to a recognition by the Church that an act was in itself sufficiently gruelling to serve as full penance. It became increasingly important to lay down with precision the terms of service expected of a *crucesignatus*. There was for example the problem of Crusaders who died before their period of service was complete: did they gain the indulgence or not? There were others who took the Cross but let years go by without leaving for the East; according to complaints lodged with the Pope, some used their immunity from the secular courts to commit serious crimes. Other privileges which had accrued to the status of Crusader were valuable, especially the moratorium on interest payments and the postponement of legal proceedings: individuals deep in debt or facing difficult court cases took the Cross to gain a respite from their problems, so practicable means of enforcing their Crusade vows (of which heritability was one) had to be worked out.

Another development whose consequences forced canon lawyers to think hard was Innocent III's extension of the indulgence to non-participants. It followed quite naturally that once the close association of crusading with pilgrimage was broken and the indulgence was bestowed in exchange for service, the range of services could be broadened far beyond personal combat. Innocent established that a full indulgence could be earned in exchange for sending a deputy, and he also made indulgences available to people who contributed a ship. Purely financial contributions were rewarded with partial indulgences, depicted as specified periods of time, which the contributor would not have to spend suffering purgatory's torments. More radical were provisions made by the Pope during the preaching of the Fifth Crusade. Innocent encouraged the 'redemption' or buying back of vows by people who took the Cross, but were later judged unfit to serve in person and were too poor to send a deputy. They could receive the full indulgence, together with all the privileges of the *crucesignatus*, in exchange for a simple financial payment. Innocent has been criticized for degrading the devotional practice of crusading by associating its full spiritual benefit with the handing over of cash, albeit coupled with the standard procedures of confession and absolution. Viewed from another perspective, however, it was a process of democratization, making the spiritual gifts of crusading available to the entire population rather than just its élite. Women in particular, who had formerly been on the margins of the crusading experience, were now brought fully within its reach. As one model sermon put it, 'during the time when the Cross is preached the flood-gates of heaven stand open for an abundance of indulgences, Mother Church opens her arms and extends her hands to the poor'.

Undoubtedly this new approach caused a number of serious problems. One was that the enthusiasm aroused by effective preaching by men like Bernard of Clairvaux and Fulk of Neuilly, or Oliver of Paderborn in the case of the Fifth Crusade, could not simply be channelled into financial payments and liturgical activities such as Masses and processions. Outbursts like the 'Children's Crusade' and the *Pastoureaux* represented the viewpoint, held with burning conviction by the poor, that they were God's chosen instruments and that it was through them, rather than through the more wealthy, that Jerusalem was to be regained. This view was strengthened by the Church's interpretation of crusading failure as the punishment for sin: for as Cléry and Villehardouin had observed during the Fourth Crusade, it was the nobles and senior ecclesiastics whose pride, greed and ambition laid them open to the key vices. Secondly, the availability of indulgences for staying at home undercut recruitment, tempting able-bodied fighting men to redeem their vows rather than embarking on the arduous and hazardous journey to the East. And bringing cash into the preaching of the Crusades naturally opened up the possibility of fraudulent practices by preachers, both genuine and false ones.

Innocent's approach towards the Crusade was ingenious to the extent that it simultaneously addressed the problem of funding (which the events of the Fourth Crusade had brought so much to the foreground), the need to make crusading militarily effective and the Pope's concern to make best use of the massive yearning amongst his contemporaries to see Jerusalem regained and to enjoy the spiritual benefits of crusading. The scope and audacity of his approach towards the instruments of crusading were formidable, and as with all such grand projects the devil lay in the detail. This was to test the finest minds of the papal court, and crusading enthusiasts outside it, throughout the thirteenth century and beyond. But nobody seriously considered either turning the clock back to the days of the armed pilgrimage *en masse*, or excluding the vast majority of Europe's population from the enterprise.

For good or ill, Innocent III's circle had brought crusading up to date in a society which was much more urbanized, commercial and diverse than that known by Pope Urban II. This entailed its becoming more institutional and legal in nature. 'Ad liberandam', the canon passed at the Fourth Lateran Council in 1215 on behalf of the Fifth Crusade, encapsulated the trend – it set out the rights and privileges of *crucesignati* so comprehensively and magisterially that it was referred to on numerous occasions for more than three centuries. Charles Péguy's dictum that 'tout commence en mystique et finit en politique' ('everything starts mystical and ends up political'), has been quoted to support the argument that crusading paid a price for this refinement by losing much of its devotional nature. This is a judgement so sweeping that it is not capable of being proved or disproved. What is undeniable is that the armies of preachers, especially members of the new mendicant orders, Franciscans and Dominicans, who called on the population to take the Cross in the thirteenth century, were accompanied or followed by armies of collectors who had the unenviable task of compelling clerics to pay taxes imposed by the Pope on behalf of the Crusade. In this respect crusading certainly became big business: donations, legacies and vow redemption payments could be expected to do no more than 'top up' the money raised from crusading's cash cow, which was the ordinary income of churchmen taxed, usually at a rate of 10%, for a number of consecutive years. The proceeds were granted to individuals of high rank who had taken the Cross and had the status and experience needed to raise men, supplies and shipping, and lead them to the East. This too was not without its difficulties, replicating at the level of command the problem of enforcement which existed in the case of each individual's Crusade vow. The problem began at the top: the Emperor Frederick II was far from being the last ruler to be excommunicated for a delay in carrying out a Crusade vow.

The work of these unsung (and largely unpaid) cohorts of preachers and collectors represented only one way in which European society experienced the Crusade in the thirteenth century. Another was through the preparations made by individuals who took the Cross. At no time had more than a small percentage of Europe's population in any given generation actually gone on Crusade: in the case of the First Crusade a very rough estimate may be made that about one person in 500 (0.2%) took part. There was an exceptional amount of crusading in the course of the thirteenth century but Europe's population had increased by about 70% since 1095. So as in the case of the First Crusade the impact on most people's lives was indirect and consequential, the result of husbands, kinfolk, neighbours and lords taking the Cross. As always, these people had much to do before departure. Money had to be raised by selling or pledging assets like farms, woods, fish-ponds, rents and market or bridge tolls, or raising loans on future income. Permissions had to be sought for absence and arrangements made for essential duties to be carried out by others. Provision had to be made for the eventuality of death while on Crusade. What had changed since the First Crusade was the greater intricacy of social affairs and the seemingly inexorable advance of government. In the thirteenth century royal courts and officials had to be taken into account by *crucesignati* as they set about these preparations. They could present insuperable obstacles if an individual's absence was perceived as being contrary to the King's will, for in the eyes of the career-bureaucrats and civil lawyers who staffed Europe's administrations, service to the King came before service to Christ. This is perhaps harsh (service to Christ was, after all, a voluntary act), and to a large degree crusading came to depend on the help of these bureaucrats and lawyers, who pursued dilatory *crucesignati*, enforced contracts for crusading, and commuted prison sentences into military service in the Holy Land. Joinville has an interesting example of this latter practice, recounting how, shortly before St Louis's first Crusade, three men robbed a clerk in Paris – their choice of victim was a poor one, because he went home to fetch weapons, doggedly tracked down his assailants and killed them all. The case came before St Louis, and it was obviously tempting to pardon the clerk outright. Instead the King took him on Crusade with him, 'because I wish my people to understand that I will never uphold them in any of their misdeeds'.

The constitution of crusading armies in the thirteenth century remained diverse, but in a different way from those of the early Crusades. Instead of presenting us with a fair cross-section of contemporary society, the poor, knights, magnates and clerics joined by their common vow of pilgrimage, they reflected the different recruitment techniques employed. There were *crucesignati*, like Joinville, who were funding themselves and others; men who were serving for pay or as deputies, who may or may not have taken the Cross; personnel contributed by the Military Orders, both serving brethren and hired troops; convicted criminals serving their time; and finally contingents fielded by the region's leading lay powers, such as the 400 knights led by the Prince of Morea (the Peloponnese), William of Villehardouin, and the Count of Jaffa's galley, so vividly described by Joinville. It is very striking, however, that despite this important shift away from pilgrimage, the Crusaders' devotional lives remained firmly focused on a perception of themselves as penitential pilgrims. Joinville constantly refers to the King's Crusades as pilgrimages even though neither involved visiting a shrine of major significance; the second Crusade, for example, he described as 'the pilgrimage of the Cross'. The rites involved in crusading were still clearly those of pilgrimage. Joinville's own preparations were typical of many: he sent for the saintly Abbot of Cheminon who gave him the traditional pilgrim staff and wallet, then left the castle of Joinville on foot, humbly dressed, proceeding first to local shrines to venerate the relics and, doubtless, to beg the saints for their intercession on his behalf. It was a mirror image of procedures followed by the King himself.

The penitential tone was maintained on Crusade. Of course some allowance has to be made for Joinville's hagiographic agenda, as well as for the fact that Joinville himself was unusually pious. At intervals during the *VdsL* individuals and groups are mentioned who failed to meet up to the exacting standards set by the King and his circle. To the King's horror, prostitutes practised their trade not very far from the royal tent and on one occasion Louis became furious when he found out that his brother Charles of Anjou was gambling. Joinville tells a revealing story of how he rebuked six of his own knights who were chatting loudly while a Mass was being celebrated for a dead comrade: his temper did not improve when he found out that they were speculating on who would marry the man's widow. We should not read too much into such incidents, which were hardly without precedent. Joinville supplies other anecdotes that show an overwhelming urge to repent arising from the brutal behaviour which remained part of the knight's existence in the mid-thirteenth century, though less so than it had been at the time of the First Crusade. He gives a first-hand account of his uncle, Josserand de Brancion, who became involved in an armed clash within a church on a Good Friday. At its close Brancion fell to his knees at the altar and emotionally beseeched Christ 'to take me out of these wars among Christians in which I have spent a great part of my life, and grant that I may die in your service, and so come to enjoy your kingdom in paradise'.

The penitential atmosphere in which the King strove to conduct his Crusade was at its strongest when setbacks occurred. The King subscribed to the view that failure was caused by sinfulness. Joinville of course agreed – the denouement of his story about the six disrespectful knights was that God exacted his vengeance on them by felling them all in battle the very next day. Making blatant use of hindsight, Joinville depicted the papal legate complaining about the sinfulness of Acre's inhabitants. One day, he predicted, with clear reference to the port's fall in 1291, the people of Acre would pay for their misdeeds. One response to serious defeats, which was as old as the First Crusade, was to embark on elaborate displays of collective penance. Processions were organized to secure God's favour when it was feared that a part of the army commanded by the King's brother Alphonse of Poitiers had suffered disaster at sea. More broadly, however, the King's approach was to take the blame on his own shoulders and to incorporate penance into his day-to-day existence.

The devotional experience of crusading in St Louis's time therefore remained strongly in harmony with that of earlier generations. Yet there were also signs of a significant shift in thinking. Here again Joinville makes an excellent guide. Towards the start of the *VdsL* he tells the story of an occasion at Corbeil when Robert de Sorbon, the royal chaplain, rebuked Joinville in front of the King for being more finely dressed than Louis. Joinville turned the tables on Robert by pointing out that his own garment, a fur-trimmed green cloth, was a sign of the status he inherited from his parents, whereas the surcoat worn by Sorbon, the son of commoners, was made of better quality cloth than the King's. Dress should reflect standing and ancestry, a point on which Joinville claimed Louis privately supported him. This emphasis on display matching status, and the wholly acceptable pride in lineage that went with it, is evident in Joinville's admiring description of his kinsman, the Count of Jaffa's galley at Damietta:

> 'his galley was covered, both under and above the water, with painted escutcheons bearing his arms, which are *or* with a Cross of *gules patée*. He had at least three hundred rowers in his galley; beside each rower was a small shield with the Count's arms upon it, and to each shield was attached a pennon with the same arms worked in gold.'

When such attitudes were taken on Crusade, they were inevitably at odds with the humility and self-abasement of the pilgrim. The problem went back

20. Effigy of Richard I from his tomb at Fontevraud.

a long way: it is already present in the arguments which contemporaries constructed to account for the failure of the Crusaders who went East in 1101 in the immediate aftermath of the First Crusade. Pride and vanity were stock charges levelled against the nobility. But certain trends in the mid-thirteenth century made the tension more telling. In the first place, it was an age of conspicuous expenditure and of delight in show, hence the didactic point of the Robert de Sorbon anecdote. Secondly, much crusading enthusiasm flowed from awareness of ancestral participation in previous Crusades – it was difficult to disentangle family pride from a more sober sense of inherited responsibility. Most importantly however, the bestowal of the Crusader's rewards, spiritual and material, in exchange for service, made it natural for men from Joinville's class to place what they did in the context of chivalric duty. The Church had always accepted that the crusading message had to be tailored to fit the thinking of the aristocracy. We have seen that language couched in feudal terms, focusing on the Crusader as Christ's vassal summoned to perform his military obligations in defence of his lord's patrimony, was deployed from the start. Such language remained popular in the thirteenth century, but increasingly it was being generalized into a knightly duty towards God. The appeal was directed as fully at the knight as at the penitent Christian, what was demanded as much the courageous performance of professional skills as a pious display of repentance.

Joinville celebrates with exuberance knighthood, *courtoisie*, and the respect for noble-born ladies, which lay at the heart of the chivalric code. One of his most vivid descriptions is of the fully armed and ferocious Gautier de Châtillon riding from end to end of a village street in Egypt repelling successive bands of Turks, yelling his battle cry and calling for his men: 'Châtillon, knights! Where are my *prud'hommes*?' During the battle of Mansurah he recounts how the Count of Soissons, hard-pressed by the Turks, yelled at him 'seneschal, let these dogs howl as they will. By God's bonnet we shall talk of this day yet, you and I, sitting at home with our ladies.' While on Cyprus, *en route* to Egypt, he heard that Marie de Brienne, the Empress of Constantinople, was at Paphos desperately seeking help for the Latin empire, and that thanks to the temporary loss of her ship she had nothing to wear except the clothes she was dressed in. This was grist to the chivalric mill. Joinville immediately dispatched Marie cloth for a dress, and together with many others he bound himself on oath to go to her assistance at Constantinople once the Crusade had finished, provided an expeditionary force was put together (i.e. somebody else paid). With such stories and somewhat stagy commitments we are entering a world presaged at times by

Villehardouin, but fundamentally different from that known by the author of the *Gesta Francorum*. The Crusade was becoming, in Joinville's phrase, 'the service of God and the King overseas'. Penitence and chivalry are held in a fine balance, in much the same way that St Louis advised that a nobleman's clothing and armour should be: 'of such a kind that men of mature experience will not say that we have spent too much on them, nor younger men say we have spent too little'.

Louis IX's own assumption of the Cross in 1244 defies any straightforward explanation. Joinville gives what had clearly become the accepted account, that it was a thank-offering for recovery from a life-threatening illness: 'as soon as he was able to speak he asked for the Cross to be given him; and this was promptly done'. The situation in the Latin East had degenerated from serious to catastrophic: the Khwarismian Turks, hired by the Sultan of Egypt, as-Salih, to fight for him against the rival Sultans of Damascus, Homs and Aleppo, seized Jerusalem from the Franks in August 1244. The authorities of the kingdom of Jerusalem allied with the Syrian Sultans against Egypt and suffered a defeat at La Forbie, near Gaza, in October 1244. La Forbie was a disaster on the scale of Hattin (1187), the Military Orders in particular suffering the loss of nearly all the troops they fielded. These events made a new Crusade imperative, but the most Louis could have been aware of when he took the Cross was the loss of Jerusalem. There had been a substantial French Crusade to Palestine in 1239–41 and Louis may have felt that the French Crown had been absent from the East for too long. He knew that he could safely leave the kingdom in the hands of his mother Blanche of Castile. But all this is speculative. All we can say with certainty is that, as one historian has expressed it, the Crusade 'quickly became the fundamental vehicle for his profound piety'.

The King's preparations for his Crusade lasted nearly three and a half years. Joinville tells us little about them, but the French monarchy had developed a sophisticated administration which has left enough traces for us to conclude that it was the best organized Crusade since that of Richard Coeur de Lion. Quite possibly Louis's crusading army was the finest which ever left for the East, which, of course, made its defeat all the more crushing. Louis's concern, to use a phrase coined by a recent biographer, focused on 'moral preoccupations and material efficiency'. The chief moral preoccupation was to remedy any injustices committed in his name, so that the pilgrimage would work its full benefit. Joinville wrote that at Easter 1248 he summoned all his vassals and asked them to present their grievances. 'My friends', he depicted himself saying, 'I'm soon going oversea, and I don't know whether

I shall ever return, so if I have done you any wrong I will make it good, to each of you in turn'. The King had already done the same on a national scale. Investigators called *enquêteurs*, for the most part Franciscan and Dominican friars, were sent out early in 1247, and the governmental abuses they uncovered brought about a wave of sackings in the higher ranks of the administration. Such a systematic purging of the royal conscience before setting out for the East was unprecedented.

'Material efficiency' meant largely two things, the first being solvency. The King ended up spending over £1,500,000 *tournois* on his Crusade, and nearly two-thirds of this sum came from taxes levied on the French Church. This was a massive vindication of Innocent III's belief that the Church could and should bear the costs of crusading, though the complaints of churchmen were loud and long. Their enthusiasm for the *negotium Christi* was seriously affected, though this mattered less than it might have done since the task of preaching was now entrusted largely to the mendicant friars. About a half of the remaining money was donated by towns in the royal domain, the rest coming from more miscellaneous sources. These included goods confiscated from Jews and convicted heretics, features of the King's religious belief which have proved less palatable to modern admirers than his generosity to the poor. Louis was so well-funded that it was only five years after departure that he had to start borrowing. This financial buoyancy was important in part because it enabled the King to bail out those barons who ran out of money and petitioned to be taken into royal pay. One example was Joinville himself and his following of eleven men. When the crusading army reached Cyprus Joinville had only 240 *livres* (pounds) *tournois* left. Louis came to his rescue with 800 *livres*.

Louis's financial planning was impressive; even more so was his construction of an embarkation port at Aigues-Mortes. Shipping was not a problem: the King contracted for twenty ships from Marseilles and sixteen from Genoa, and there were ample vessels for Crusaders like Joinville to make their own arrangements without difficulty. The obvious port to use was Marseilles, but the King was anxious to leave for the East from a port situated within the royal domain and Marseilles lay in his brother Charles's lands in Provence. Aigues-Mortes was no more than a fishing village, but Louis had already started to build on its potential before taking the Cross, and a vast amount of money and administrative energy was poured into it in 1245–8 to equip it with the facilities, supplies and fresh water adequate for an army numbering several thousand men. Although only one stone building of any size, the *Tour de Constance*, had been constructed by the time Louis arrived at Aigues-

Mortes, the overall project is a striking testimony to his government's efficiency. Of equal importance was the geography involved, for Aigues-Mortes lay in the far south, in a region hundreds of miles from the centre of Capetian power in the Paris basin, and only recently brought under royal control.

In all of this the Pope, Innocent IV, was little more than an observer. Innocent was almost fully preoccupied with his conflict with Emperor Frederick II. It ended only with Frederick's death in 1250 and its ramifications in Germany and Italy were profound. Innocent issued Crusade bulls, galvanized and coerced the French clergy as much as he could, and attempted, unsuccessfully, to tax the Church in other lands on behalf of Louis's Crusade. The Pope was not in a position to do more and despite the disaster at La Forbie he regarded the struggle against Frederick II as enjoying priority: Louis had to work hard to stop the papal-imperial dispute from encroaching on his preparations. This strengthened the tendency for the expedition to be both planned and executed as, overwhelmingly, a French Crusade. Some Scots and English knights took part in the expedition and a Norwegian force arrived in the East in 1250, too late to assist in the Egyptian campaign; Joinville describes with admiration the skill and bravery which the Norwegians showed in hunting lions (with which they can hardly have been familiar) in Syria. The rest of the army was French. It consisted of between 2,500 and 2,800 knights, 5,000 squires and sergeants, and about 10,000 foot soldiers.

The army embarked at the end of August 1248. One effect of La Forbie was to strengthen the strategy, projected for the Fourth Crusade and pursued by the Fifth, of attacking 'the serpent's head' in Egypt. Louis decided to make his assault in the spring of 1249 from Cyprus, and with that in mind sent ahead agents to purchase and transport substantial supplies so that his army would lack for nothing while wintering on the island. The results of their activities were plain to see when the French arrived in September, not least in the form of the great heaps of wheat and barley which were stored near Limassol. These provided Joinville with perhaps his most famous passage, in which he described how rain had made the corn on top sprout, so the heaps looked like hills; when this surface vegetation was peeled away the grain underneath was found to be in excellent condition. What should have been an easy winter turned out to be anything but, for the French army was decimated by disease. However, the stay enabled Louis to gather news about the rapidly changing situation in the Middle East. Predictably, La Forbie had effected a decisive shift in the balance of power amongst the Ayyubids to the advantage of as-Salih of Egypt, enabling him to occupy Damascus, but of equal importance was the advance of the Mongols in the East. Hoping that the Great Khan might be favourable to an alliance against the Muslims, Louis dispatched envoys with impressive gifts.

On 13 May 1249 the fleet sailed from Limassol; 'it was', Joinville commented, 'a lovely sight to look at, for it seemed as if all the sea, as far as the eye could reach, was covered with the canvas of the ships' sails'. Like the leaders of the Fifth Crusade, Louis decided to attack Damietta, but unlike his predecessors he enjoyed a spectacular stroke of good fortune. Sultan as-Salih had expected an attack here and garrisoned Damietta with élite troops, Banu Kinana Arabs. However, the initial landing caused confusion and panic, and after some hard fighting on the beaches the garrison withdrew southward. Damietta was occupied at the cost of few casualties. What followed was highly revealing in terms of crusading attitudes. Damietta itself Louis treated as his conquest, to be disposed of exactly as he wished. Thus he converted the Great Mosque into a cathedral and made endowments to it. He also instructed his officials to charge high prices for the lease of shops to merchants, and he set aside all the grain in Damietta for the victualling of his army. The measures on shop premises and grain disturbed Joinville – the first he considered counter-productive in terms of the promotion of victualling in the long run since it deterred merchants, while the second ran counter to 'the good old custom' that captured grain, like any type of booty, was subject to general distribution once the King had taken his third. The situation reminds one of Cléry's complaints about the baronial leadership of the Fourth Crusade in 1204 – they too had been accused of short-changing the rank and file. It is striking to find much the same charge being levelled against St Louis, especially as he was usually very scrupulous about respecting custom. Of course one answer might be that the King was looking to the best interests of his army.

There remains his treatment of the town of Damietta. In regarding it as newly acquired property of the French Crown Louis was himself applying the customary law of conquest, like the leaders of the First Crusade at Antioch, Richard I and Philip II at Acre, and the Crusaders at Constantinople in 1204. Louis displayed few signs of greed or acquisitiveness on a personal level, except where relics were concerned, but he was always very mindful of the prerogatives attaching to his status as King of France; in that capacity he was certainly not going to let the port slip out of his grasp. What is less easy to read is his thinking about the future in the long term of Damietta and any other conquests which he made in Egypt. The endowment of a cathedral was not the action of a ruler who was planning to exchange his conquests for a defensible enclave in Palestine, so it has been suggested that Louis's interpretation of the Egyptian strategy accorded with that of the papal legate Pelagius on the Fifth Crusade. Pelagius had staked everything on the conquest of the whole Nile Delta, and Louis may have intended to do the same; it is possible that he even envisaged a French kingdom of Egypt to be ruled by one of his sons. Some years later he would have no objection to the Pope enfeoffing his brother Charles with the kingdom of Sicily. This was more than naked dynasticism: Louis was obsessed with the idea of conversion and at this point entertained heady hopes of winning over the Mongols to Christ. If christianized Mongols conquered Syria while Louis himself overran Egypt, Islam in the Middle East would come close to extinction. In that context the winning back of Jerusalem would not be an end in itself but the coping stone on an architecture of achievement which surpassed even the First Crusade.

In applying the crusading strategy of attacking Egypt the attempt to capture a port was never the cause of Christian defeat; it was always the next stage which brought failure. The rapid success at Damietta offered the opportunity of an immediate march on Cairo. This would capitalize on Muslim demoralization but it would have to be quick if the French were not to be caught out by the flooding of the Nile which took place in early summer. Louis regarded the risk as too great, and he used the excuse of waiting for his brother Alphonse, Count of Poitiers, to postpone the advance until the autumn of 1249. It was not until 20 November that the laborious march southward began. A month later the army reached the banks of the Bahr as-Saghir, the Nile tributary which makes its way to Lake Manzalah and barred the approach from the north to the key fortress-town of Mansurah. Weeks were spent in constructing a causeway and bridge over the Bahr as-Saghir in the face of ferocious Muslim resistance, notable for the highly effective use made of naphtha (*naft*, 'Greek fire'). Progress was poor when on 2 February 1250 Louis's constable, Humbert of Beaujeu, revealed that a Bedouin convert was prepared to show the Crusaders the location of a ford downstream from their camp. Here a crossing was forced on 8 February and the Crusaders stormed into the Egyptian camp, scattering the opposition. But the King's brother, Robert of Artois, would not stop here, leading his men in a headlong pursuit into Mansurah itself. The tightest discipline thus proved ineffective in the face of one individual's blind folly. In Mansurah's narrow streets the Crusaders were cut off and cut down. The Templars alone lost 280 knights. The provost of the Hospitallers gave the King the news of his brother's death in a touching scene:

'"Ah, your majesty, take comfort in the thought that no king of France has gained such honour as you have gained today. For, in order to fight your enemies, you swam across a river, to rout them utterly and drive them from the field. Besides this, you have captured their machines, and also their tents, in which you will be sleeping tonight." "May God be worshipped for all he has given me", replied the King; and then big tears began to fall from his eyes.'

Mansurah remained in Muslim hands, and they were particularly capable ones, because the garrison's commander was Baybars al-Bunduqdari, a man generally acknowledged to have surpassed even Saladin in his capacity for conquest. On 11 February Baybars tested the mettle of the Crusaders in a pitched battle which brought heavy losses to both sides. Joinville describes both this encounter and its predecessor on 8 February in rich detail; his emphasis is naturally on the deeds of the knights, but it is apparent that the royal crossbowmen also fought with exceptional skill and courage. The problem was that the crusading army grew weaker while Baybars was being reinforced. Even the death of as-Salih while his heir Turanshah was in Syria had not helped the Crusaders, for Turanshah's mother Shajar al-Durr had handled the transition of power smoothly. The French suffered the onset of an epidemic caused by eating polluted river fish. They also found that food supplies stopped arriving from their base at Damietta. The Muslims had loaded dismantled galleys onto camels, taken these to the rear of Louis's army, and launched the rebuilt galleys on the Nile. Cut off from their source of supply, the Crusaders soon faced that all-too familiar problem of crusading armies operating in the East, famine conditions. Just as during similar scenarios in the First and Fourth Crusades, Joinville registered the severity of the famine in terms of the inflated prices which food commanded, from £30 for a pig to 12d for an egg.

Mansurah could not be taken now, so the only option was retreat, first across the Bahr as-Saghir and then, with painful slowness due to the number of sick, northward along the bank of the Nile. This was Louis's *via dolorosa*. He was always very sensitive to his army's suffering: when *naphtha* was being hurled at the French he had sat up in bed, raised his hands in prayer and exclaimed, weeping, 'Gracious Lord, guard my people for me'. He himself had contracted the epidemic and was also suffering badly from dysentery, but he refused to board a ship and was carried in the army's rearguard. In circumstances of great confusion, and probable treachery, the King was taken

21. Coin of Edward I 1272–1307.

prisoner, and most of his army soon followed him into captivity. Joinville was captured when his ship was taken, coming close to losing his life in the process; he was saved by the quick-thinking of a Muslim from Sicily who decided it was in his interests to look after this high-ranking Frank.

There were no established laws of war regulating what should happen to captives on either side and many of the Crusaders were killed outright by the Muslims, or given the choice between conversion and execution. Gradually Turanshah exerted control over the situation and negotiations for release began. Initially the Sultan hoped to coerce the French into handing over the remaining Frankish possessions in the Holy Land in exchange for their freedom. When he realized that this was impracticable he fell back on the return of Damietta and a cash sum of £400,000. But no sooner had the details been ratified than the captives found themselves caught up in a palace revolution. Since Seljuq times Muslim armies had included large numbers of slave soldiers, the *mamluks*. Many were Kipchak Turks, originating in the southern Russian steppe lands, Crimea and the Caucasus, captured or bought while young and converted to Islam by their owners. Some, such as Baybars, rose to positions of command, which brought them not just personal freedom but wealth and status. A group of these amirs, promoted by as-Salih, feared that Turanshah's arrival would spell the end of their influence if not of their careers, and they assassinated the Sultan on 2 May. Their approach towards the French captives was by no means certain and, anticipating death, Louis's barons went so far as to hear each other's confessions. But the assassins stood by the terms of release agreed with Turanshah. St Louis was released and on 6 May he reached the safety of a Genoese galley, his unhindered embarkation ensured by the trigger fingers of eighty crossbowmen with loaded bolts.

The King sailed not for Limassol but for Acre, thereby making it clear that despite all his losses in men, money and matériel he had not made up his mind to abandon his Crusade. It was a courageous stance to take, and at Acre, in the face of letters from his mother beseeching him to return, and strong lobbying to the same effect from most of his barons, Louis resolved to stay in the Holy Land. 'Many of those who heard these words were filled with amazement, and many there were who wept.' The King had two goals, which he set out in a newsletter sent home for circulation among his subjects. One was to secure the release of the Crusaders still in captivity, about which the new rulers of Egypt were proving dilatory in meeting their obligations; and the other was to do all he could to bolster the existing defences of the kingdom of Jerusalem. These were limited objectives, compared with the grand plans pursued just a few months previously, but the resources available were also much smaller; the King's surviving brothers and most of his magnates sailed home and Louis was left with a few dozen enthusiasts like Joinville, whose services had to be supplemented by troops hired on the spot. It is unlikely that that he ever had more than 500 knights under his command. Nonetheless, the three and a half years which the King remained in the Holy Land must be regarded not as an aftermath to his Crusade but as its second phase: less ambitious and maybe less heroic than the months spent in Egypt but just as purposeful. Louis himself certainly saw his status in the Holy Land not as an honoured guest but the overall leader of the Christian war effort, exercising authority over the barons of the kingdom as well as over the Military Orders. When the Marshal of the Templars engaged in negotiations with Damascus without consulting Louis, the King's reaction was harsh; the Master was subjected to a public humiliation and the Marshal banished from the kingdom of Jerusalem.

Louis achieved both of his objectives, and in the course of doing so he confirmed what was already becoming clear, that small-scale military action coupled with diplomatic finesse often delivered more results than major expeditions like that to Egypt. The freeing of the prisoners was only brought about after protracted wrangling and it is likely that as many died in prison as were released. The work on the kingdom's defences was approached in a very systematic fashion. First came the building of a wall enclosing Acre's extensive suburb of Montmusard, in 1250–1. This was followed by massive rebuilding at Caesarea, the port south of Acre, which Saladin had dismantled in 1191. The King then turned his attention to Jaffa, where Joinville remembered him carrying the earth himself in order to gain the indulgences offered for manual work. Finally the defences of Sidon were strengthened. In all probability more than £100,000 were spent on these projects. When building work at Sidon was completed, in February 1254, Louis made preparations to leave for France, embarking at Acre in April. As significant as what he did was what he did not do, which was to visit Jerusalem. In 1251 Louis was on very good terms with the Ayyubid Sultan of Aleppo, al-Nasir, who controlled the holy places. The King visited Nazareth for the Feast of the Annunciation but declined the chance to visit Jerusalem. Following the precedent of Richard I on the Third Crusade, he argued that if he visited the city while it was in Muslim hands, it would set a bad example, leading others to prefer the comparatively easy option of pilgrimage to the complex task of military recovery.

Although Louis could hardly be expected to know it, the Middle East, which he left behind him in April 1254, was in the throes of the most far-reaching change since the arrival of the Seljuq Turks in the eleventh century. Two dynamic new military powers had appeared on the scene and their conflict would implicate the Franks and end by sweeping them aside. The first power was that of the governmental system set up in Egypt by Turanshah's rebellious *mamluks* after they assassinated the Ayyubid Sultan in 1250. The dynasty founded by Saladin never regained power in Egypt. Aybek, the man elected by the conspirators, first as commander-in-chief and later as Sultan, was himself a former *mamluk*, and his successors emerged from among the same officer class, as often as not through bloody coups. The Mamluk regime was an oligarchy, much more centralized than the Ayyubid family 'federation', and it revived the ideals and objectives of *jihad*, to which Saladin's successors had been content to pay lip-service. Many of the Mamluks were fervent Muslims, predisposed to be hostile to the Franks on religious grounds, and they commanded the military resources to be a very dangerous enemy. Their emphasis on highly trained and well-equipped cavalry units enabled them to confront the Franks on the battlefield with confidence, and they approached siege warfare with unusual ingenuity and persistence.

The second new military power was the Mongols. St Louis's envoy to the Golden Horde, Andrew of Longjumeau, returned while the King was in the

Holy Land, and it was clear that as things stood the hope of an alliance with the Mongols was misplaced – their reply showed that they were interested only in submission. Soon after the King sailed home Hülegü Khan, Chinggis Khan's grandson, led a westward thrust of astonishing violence. Cities were destroyed and regimes which had seemed rock hard were toppled overnight. In 1256 Hülegü annihilated the Assassins at Alamut, and two years later he brought to an end the ancient Abbasid caliphate at Baghdad. In 1260 he invaded Syria and pillaged Aleppo. This was an unprecedented challenge to Islam's hegemony in the Middle East, and it was conducted with a ferocity and speed that far surpassed any of the crusading armies. The Mamluks rose to the defence of their embattled faith and in September 1260 defeated the Mongols at the battle of Ayn Jalut, south of the Sea of Galilee. The Mongols withdrew, and soon afterwards their empire fragmented into a number of khanates, including the *Ilkhanate* which controlled Iraq, Iran, and much of Anatolia. The *Ilkhans* showed periodic interest in an alliance with the Franks but it never proceeded beyond the stage of envoys being exchanged.

Hülegü's invasion of Syria was disastrous for the Franks. It brought to an end the relatively manageable strategic scenario which had existed since Saladin's death in 1193. That scenario had been badly disturbed by the battle of La Forbie and even more so by the Mamluk coup of 1250. The diplomacy conducted by St Louis while he was in the Holy Land had demonstrated that it was still possible to play off the Mamluks against the Ayyubid Princes of Syria. The destruction carried out by the Mongols, on the other hand, followed by their own rapid withdrawal after Ayn Jalut, left a power vacuum in Syria, which the Mamluks were both well-placed and anxious to fill. In 1260 Baybars, the victor of Mansurah, murdered the reigning Sultan and seized power. Baybars went on immediately to seize Damascus and to create a member of the Abbasid family as caliph in Egypt, thereby associating the centre of Mamluk military power with Sunni orthodoxy. The new caliph invested Baybars both with the lands which he already held and with those further east in Mongol hands. The diploma of investiture dwelt on the obligation of *jihad*, reflecting and reinforcing the Mamluks' perception of themselves as champions of Islam, and in turn strengthening their hostility towards the Franks. There was a powerful strategic reason too for them to undertake the total reconquest of Palestine and northern Syria for Islam: this was the fear of another great Crusade being launched in conjunction with a renewed Mongol offensive. There was an urgency in the Mamluk assaults on the Franks which had no precedent in the way Islamic leaders in the past had responded to the Latin states, even in the time of Nur al-Din and Saladin.

Joinville was fascinated by both the Mongols and the Mamluks, and showed himself to be especially well-informed on the constitution of the Mamluk armies. What lay at the heart of his interest in both groups was his zest for the unusual, which certainly did not stop at religious boundaries. It is clear that in Joinville's world the understanding of the Muslim enemy had reached a much more sophisticated level than at the time of the First Crusade. Indeed it would have been astonishing if it had not given a century and a half of interaction between Franks and Muslims in the Middle East. One of the most readable sections of Joinville's text is that on the captivity of the French, when, as in most prison narratives, circumstances exposed them to the extremes of human behaviour. Actual or threatened massacres are juxtaposed with striking instances of *courtoisie* and kindness, even if the latter was motivated in part by self-interest. Joinville paid tribute to Islamic medicine, which cured him of a throat illness so severe that he feared death. And he follows this with a touching story of an old Muslim knight who used to carry one of Joinville's disabled companions on his back to the privy. When Joinville inadvertently ate meat on a Friday, it was his Muslim captor who sensibly pointed out that this could not be construed as a sin since he had simply lost track of time in the confusion of the retreat.

The mutual need to exact oaths that the ransom arrangements would be honoured is particularly revealing of how much Christians and Muslims knew about each other's religious beliefs. The Mamluk amirs swore three oaths. One was to the effect that non-observance would be as shameful as an act for which penance would require a pilgrimage to Mecca with uncovered head. The others equated the shame of betraying the oath with that of taking back a wife who had been repudiated, and of eating pork. Clumsily phrased though they were, the oaths show a grasp of how far Muslim society incorporated concepts of shame and dishonour which were recognizable to Catholics and could be harnessed to their uses. The Muslims had greater difficulties with the King's oath. He was content to swear an oath equating betrayal with apostasy and excommunication, but drew the line at the very suggestion, implicit in the whole procedure, that he might fall guilty of the third transgression, which was trampling and spitting on the Cross. To exert pressure on Louis the amirs tortured the aged patriarch of Jerusalem, and it was his suffering, combined with his assurance that the King's soul would come to no harm through the oath, that persuaded Louis to swear it in its complete form.

Nerves became very frayed during these negotiations and at one point an amir suggested that the best way to get Louis to swear the required oath would be to send the patriarch's head flying into his lap. In general, however, Muslim sources confirm Joinville's claim that the King made a favourable impression on his captors as a man of piety and wisdom who bore his captivity not just patiently but with remarkable good humour. Joinville even introduces the *topos* that the amirs were so impressed by Louis than they offered to make him sultan after Turanshah's assassination. He certainly took a place within the small group of crusading leaders whom the Muslims remembered with respect, the main others being Richard I and Frederick II. Joinville himself records Muslim sayings which paid homage to Richard as a redoubtable warrior, while for their part the Franks were already constructing their image of Richard's great foe Saladin as a wise and courteous man, whose word could be trusted. Just as the oath negotiations revealed a common ground of honour and dishonour, so these stories show the readiness of both sides to pick out certain individuals amongst their past opponents for admiration. Joinville was also aware of the Muslim habit of quoting verses from the Qur'an in support of courses of action, a procedure which they shared with both Christians and Jews.

Joinville's text is populated with a variety of individuals who functioned in different ways as go-betweens between Christians and Muslims. The oath negotiations themselves were handled on the Christian side by a priest called Nicholas of Acre who clearly had a good command of Arabic and a sound knowledge of Islamic practices, while the Muslims used the services of renegade priests. Joinville talked to one good-looking renegade from Provins, who had married an Egyptian woman and was enjoying a life of wealth and status, although (according to Joinville) his conversion was pragmatic and he was conscious of the penalty he would have to pay after death for his Faustian pact with the devil. Trade between Christian and Muslim regions was unceasing: the traveller Ibn Jubayr had commented in 1184 that:

> 'one of the astonishing things that is talked of is that though the fires of discord burn between the two parties, Muslim and Christian, two armies of them may meet and dispose themselves in battle array, and yet Muslim and Christian travellers will come and go between them without interference'.

Even the hardening of arteries which occurred from the mid-thirteenth century with the arrival of the Mamluks and Mongols did little to stop the interaction of the two communities.

But curiosity had its limits. More importantly, there are few signs on either side of anything but outright condemnation of the other's faith as misguided and false. Louis's interest in the Muslims was exclusively as potential converts, and he could conceive of nothing worse than somebody who had gone in the opposite direction. The renegade from Provins, whom Joinville talked to amicably for some time, was curtly dismissed by Louis as soon as he found out he had abandoned the faith. Louis was so concerned about potential loss of faith that he advised against anybody except expert theologians engaging in debates with the Jews. The ordinary layman who encountered somebody abusing the Christian faith 'should not attempt to defend its tenets, except with his sword, and that he should thrust into the scoundrel's belly, and as far as it will enter'. Louis's citadel-like approach towards faith was not unusual and it accorded with the views of contemporaries that the value of securing a firmer knowledge of Islam was very largely tactical: a better understanding would enable missionaries to expose its follies and thereby bring about its longed-for destruction. Nor was the situation very different among the Muslims. It has been shown that their interest in the Franks was for the most part stimulated by alarm at their invasion of the territories of Islam (the *Dar-al-Islam*) and by a concern to discover their weaknesses and expel them. On both sides not just stereotypes but deep misunderstandings remained because of this shared premise of condemnation.

It was predictable that Louis IX would not simply put crusading behind him when he disembarked in July 1254 at Hyères. The preparation and execution of the Crusade had been too profoundly a part of his life for a full decade. Its failure he viewed chiefly in terms of his own shortcomings, both as a Christian and as the army's commander: sinful behaviour by his men was his fault because he permitted it to occur. The course of action he favoured was to enter a religious house, and although he was dissuaded from this because of the danger it might cause for the succession, his entire way of life became quasi-monastic. It has been pointed out that Louis spent heavily on display when the prestige of the Crown was involved, as on the occasion of his eldest son's being dubbed a knight in 1267. Normally, however, frugality and simplicity became the rule. Joinville narrates that Louis took no interest in the food he ate and wore undyed woollen cloth, edged not with ermine or squirrel fur but with deerskin, hare-skin or lambskin. His religious regime was strenuous: weekly confession, punishment of his body through scourging and a remarkably high level of attendance at liturgical offices. He developed a strong taste for attending the translation of saints' relics. The only luxury he allowed himself was good conversation, for he lost none of his sociability. The royal court's expenditure on the disadvantaged, especially the poor, sick and orphaned, reached exceptional heights; for the twelve months following

22. Seal of King Edward I (AD 1272–1307) on horseback and enthroned in majesty.

February 1256, for example, alms-giving absorbed close to 10% of household expenses. Every day 120 of the poor were fed in the royal household. Donations to religious houses were also generous: in Joinville's striking phrase, 'the good King Louis surrounded the city of Paris with people vowed to the service of religion'.

But Louis's reformation extended far beyond the court and Paris. Joinville summed it up succinctly when he commented that 'after King Louis had returned to France from oversea he was very devout in his worship of our Saviour and very just in his dealings with his subjects'. Medieval Europe experienced plenty of pious kings; what was distinctive about Louis after 1254 was his determination to maintain the reforming programme, which before his Crusade had been spearheaded by the *enquêteurs*. Following his return this programme became even more ambitious. The King applied his energies not just to ruling justly but to helping his subjects live full Christian lives. It was almost as if Louis was doing his best to make his people worthy of Christ, and both able and willing to respond to renewed calls to defend Christ's patrimony in the Holy Land. The King's great reforming ordinance of December 1254 became the main vehicle for these objectives. At its heart was an attempt to make royal government fairer, more efficient and accountable, through a more extensive monitoring of his officials' conduct; in future no injustice should be practised in the King's name. But this was accompanied by measures against groups who through their belief or behaviour were deemed to threaten the Christian community which it was Louis's aspiration to create, a mixed bunch comprising heretics, Jews, usurers, blasphemers, prostitutes and others. The 1254 ordinance even tried to ban the manufacture of dice in France, surely a hopeless endeavour. In general, it is extremely hard to know how much of the King's moralizing legislation had its desired effect. The most we can say is that Louis's reign was a better than average time to be poor in France, but a rather bad time to be non-Christian or unorthodox.

In the meantime the Holy Land itself was far from forgotten. The King had left a garrison of 100 knights there under the command of Geoffrey of Sergines, one of his most trusted lieutenants. So debilitated were the military resources of the Frankish establishment that Geoffrey's tiny force became important in itself. It also functioned as a symbolic link between Acre and Paris; for the beleaguered Franks in the East it was proof, daily visible, that they had not been abandoned to their fate, while for the King, and more broadly for France's nobility, it stood for their commitment to defending the Holy Land. The poet Rutebeuf devoted a poem of praise to Geoffrey, *La Complainte de Monseigneur Geoffrei de Sergines*. A steady flow of men, money and supplies made its way eastward to bolster Geoffrey's efforts. Help was needed desperately, for throughout the 1260s the news reaching the West was grim as Baybars embarked on systematic campaigns of conquest in both Palestine and Syria. The military organization available to the Sultan enabled him to be more relentless than Saladin had been able to be after Hattin. In 1263 his forces ravaged Galilee, one of his amirs destroying the church of the Nativity at Nazareth. Caesarea and Arsur fell in 1265. In 1266 Baybars took the great Templar fortress at Safad in Galilee, in 1268 Jaffa and the Templar castle of Beaufort. St Louis's arduous building work at Caesarea and Jaffa had done little to withstand the Mamluks, the former falling in two days and the latter in a single hour – even more alarming was the fall of Safad and Beaufort, which had seemed impregnable. But all such news was overshadowed by the fall of Antioch in May 1268. The city had been in Frankish hands without a break since its capture by the First Crusade in 1098; its recapture by the Muslims seemed to sound the death knell for what was left of the Christian holdings in the East.

When Antioch fell St Louis was already *crucesignatus* again. He took the Cross on the festival of the Annunciation, 25 March 1267, three of his sons including his heir, Philip, taking the Cross at the same time. The public reception of the news was distinctly mixed. The appalling outcome of the first expedition could not be forgotten. By this time the King was nearly fifty-three, old by medieval standards, and in poor health. It was quite likely that he would die on Crusade and disorder would break out in France; most people had heard stories about the baronial wars of the 1220s and 1230s and many had unpleasant memories of the *Pastoureaux* of 1251. Joinville's opinion

23. Coronation of Edward I.

of this Crusade was uncompromising: 'I considered that all those who had advised the King to go on this expedition committed mortal sin.' On the day before the King took the Cross Joinville had a dream which his chaplain interpreted to be predictive of an unsuccessful Crusade. To some extent this negative view was shaped by hindsight, but it was probably not untypical even of many who like Joinville, were predisposed to favour crusading. When Louis pressed him to take the Cross, he refused to do so on the grounds that his possessions and dependants in Champagne had suffered too much from royal oppression during his earlier absence.

> 'If I wished to do what was pleasing to God I should remain here to help and defend the people on my estates. For if, while seeing quite clearly that it would be to their detriment, I put my life in danger by venturing on this pilgrimage of the Cross, I should anger our Lord, who gave his own life to save his people.'

Such arguments against crusading were being expressed with some frequency by this point. During the preaching of Louis's Crusade Rutebeuf wrote a poem in which a *crucesignatus* argued with a knight who had refused to take the Cross: Joinville's point, that the domestic enjoyed priority, found its place here too. A few years later Humbert of Romans, the head of the Dominican Order and an experienced Crusade preacher, listed many such objections together with appropriate rejoinders so that preachers would know how to deal with them. Few of the arguments against crusading were inherently new: the historian's problem is not explaining failure to respond but the periodic resurgence of enthusiasm in the face of a past history of disasters and a sharp awareness of the ordeal that awaited Crusaders in the East. In the case of St Louis's Second Crusade, moreover, there existed the difficulty that strategic thinking was in a state of flux. The large-scale Crusade (general passage or *passagium generale*) had failed so often, and was accompanied by so many problems at home, that some enthusiasts preferred to focus on smaller expeditions of a few hundred men at most, what was beginning to be called a 'limited passage' (*passagium particulare*). There was indeed much in their favour: they were easier, quicker and less costly to organize, they could operate more effectively alongside forces raised locally, and thanks to Latin control of the sea-ways they could be disembarked wherever they were most needed. There are signs that this approach was preferred by the Latin authorities in the East. Pope Clement IV had planned just such a small expedition for the spring of 1267 and his project was thrown into confusion by news of the King's new Crusade.

24. Left: Coin of Edward I, Durham.

25. Right: Edward I Gros of Aquitaine Lion Rampant.

Clearly the problem was that no small expedition could hope to hold back the juggernaut of Mamluk military power. A few years later, Érard of Valéry commented that the Crusades of the past had been 'like the little dog barking at the big great one, who takes no heed of him' and if even the general passage could give such an impression of inferiority, how much more so would smaller forces? So St Louis planned his new venture on a large scale. We know much less about its organization than about his first expedition, but the leadership, finance and recruitment involved all lead to the conclusion that Louis conceived of it in terms no less imposing than his earlier Crusade. Apart from Louis himself it would include an impressive range of commanders: Alphonse Count of Poitiers, Edward Plantagenet, soon to become Edward I of England (who contracted for service with Louis himself in return for a loan of £70,000) King James I of Aragon and most importantly the King's brother Charles of Anjou, ruler of the kingdom of Sicily since 1266. Aragonese participation was subject to the rather volatile personality of James I and eventually it yielded little, but the additional military, financial and naval resources that Charles could bring to bear meant that, potentially at least, Louis's Crusade could be expected to match its predecessor. Whether it achieved that potential depended on Louis's ability to co-ordinate this range of French, English and Sicilian resources.

26. Top: Coin of Edward I, Canterbury.

27. Bottom: Coin of Edward I, Anglo-Gallic Lion of Gascony.

The King's plans for his Crusade were not known. This time he made no preparations for the stock-piling of supplies on Cyprus, and when he embarked at Aigues-Mortes on 1 July 1270, on ships provided by the Genoese, his destination was a secret. In the event he sailed, via Cagliari in Sardinia, to North Africa, landing near Tunis on 18 July and setting up camp on the plain of Carthage. His rationale remains unclear but the most convincing explanation was advanced by his confessor, Geoffrey of Beaulieu. This was that Louis had been informed, by an unknown source, that the Hafsid amir Mohammad was anxious to convert and required only the presence of a Christian army to give him the leverage to receive baptism and initiate the conversion of his people. The King hoped to bring this about and to proceed from Tunis to the eastern Mediterranean.

To us it appears the height of folly to begin what was in any case a problematic campaign with a preliminary landing in North Africa during one of the hottest months of the year, and on the basis of such vague hopes. Some historians have viewed the landing in Tunisia as a diversion akin to that of

28. Left: Seal for government of Scotland, Edward I, obverse.

29. Right: Seal for government of Scotland, Edward I, reverse.

the Fourth Crusade, and they have looked for a person to play the role popularly ascribed to Doge Dandolo in the case of the earlier expedition. The obvious candidate is Charles of Anjou. Like the Norman kings of Sicily before him, he had interests in Tunisia; but there is no evidence that Charles persuaded his brother to land there. Louis was not by nature a pliable individual, nor there is any need to search for such a conspiracy. For a man with Louis's intense desire to win souls, the temptation to employ his army for the purpose of conversion was irresistible. He viewed the military conflict playing itself out in Palestine and Syria as an eschatological struggle between good and evil, and probably believed that the conversion of a territory as large as Tunisia would be as fundamental a blow to Baybars as a defeat in the field. It was another version of the strategy of indirect attack, though one which is much less comprehensible to a modern way of thinking because its perspective was mystical rather than material.

The flaw was that Mohammad had no intention of converting and the Tunis venture accordingly turned into a military campaign. Louis continued to hope that the amir would make known his desire for baptism once Tunis was in Christian hands, but decided to await the arrival of his brother before attacking the city. Unsurprisingly, the army contracted disease, probably dysentery or typhus. The King himself was soon confined to his bed and died on 25 August. Charles of Anjou arrived on the same day, and his status allowed him to enforce his desire that the Crusade's Tunisian stage should be concluded by negotiations. Mohammad was concerned enough by the prospect of a Christian assault to offer generous terms in exchange for the army's withdrawal. When Edward of England arrived on 10 November, he found his fellow-Crusaders preparing to embark for Sicily, where they intended to discuss the resumption of the Crusade in the East during the spring of 1271. In the event, an extraordinarily violent storm off Trapani on 15 November inflicted such damage that only the English contingent, which appears to have escaped unharmed, was in a fit state to continue. Edward's operations around Acre in 1271–2 were thus the only outcome of St Louis's second Crusade: ironically, demonstrating once again that it was small groups of Crusaders with limited aims which had most to offer to the defence of the Holy Land.

The loss of St Louis's Crusade was deeply felt, and the Pope elected in 1271, Gregory X, was determined to do all he could to stop the momentum slackening. He summoned a general council of the Church, which met at Lyon and in 1274 passed decrees proclaiming a general passage. His actions were the most vigorous assertion of papal authority in crusading matters since the reign of Innocent III, and the conciliar decrees were modelled on those of Innocent, even to the extent of repeating much of the language. To us this sounds less than promising, but much of Innocent's basic approach remained highly relevant half a century on. Indeed one prominent feature of Innocent's policy, the imposition of a naval blockade on Egypt to deprive it of much-needed war matériel, had grown in significance with the emergence of Mamluk military power. And Gregory X was not wholly traditional in his thinking: on to the Innocentian structure he grafted some innovative ideas, including taxation measures of unprecedented range and plans for a series of advance parties which would pave the way for his general passage. In the months which followed the Lyon council Gregory made good progress with his Crusade: St Louis's successor, Philip III, took the Cross, as did his uncle Charles of Sicily and the Emperor-elect. The Pope was even prepared to accept the Byzantine reconquest of Constantinople in order to secure Greek assistance against the Mamluks.

Just a few years after Louis's death at Carthage it therefore appeared that another great expedition was about to set sail to bolster the Latin settlements in the Holy Land. But death again intervened: that of Gregory X himself in January 1276. Without the Pope working ceaselessly to push them along, his plans stalled. The way was clear for the Mamluks to complete their conquests. Baybars's attacks had slackened after 1271, partly because of the arrival of the English Crusaders but mainly because the Sultan switched his attention to the Armenians and Mongols. Baybars's death in 1277 and another Mongol invasion of Syria in 1280 gave the Franks some years of peace, and it was not until 1285 that pressure was resumed by Sultan Kalavun. His capture of Tripoli in 1289 severely alarmed the West, leading to a force of Crusaders from northern Italy arriving in Acre in the summer of 1290. Acre enjoyed a truce with Kalavun but the Crusaders provided the Mamluks with a *casus belli* by killing some Muslim peasants who had brought produce into the city to sell. Kalavun died in November 1290 and his successor, al-Ashraf Khalil, seized the opportunity to start his reign with a triumph which would match those of Saladin and Baybars: the final expulsion of the Christians. It demanded a massive effort, for Acre possessed a formidable double set of walls and failure could trigger a Crusade or bring about the Sultan's own downfall. Al-Ashraf therefore mobilized an enormous army and siege train, and took Acre in May 1291. Although a number of ports and castles were still in Frankish hands, the loss of Acre proved decisive; by the end of the summer all had capitulated except for Roche Guillaume in the far north. Almost two centuries of Christian settlement in the Levant had come to an end.

Describing St Louis's canonization, Joinville wrote that 'it has brought great honour to those of the good King's line who are like him in doing well, and equal dishonour to those descendants of his who will not follow him in good works'. These were weighty words – it is tempting to see in them a veiled reference to the shattering sequence of events which began in October 1307, exactly two years before Joinville completed the *VdsL*. This was the trial of the Templars, the series of separate juridical processes which began when Philip the Fair arrested all the French Templars, and ended when Pope Clement V decreed the order's dissolution in 1312. We shall never know Joinville's opinion on the fate of the Templars, but the trial illustrates particularly well the multi-faceted nature of St Louis's crusading legacy to his successors as kings of France. For depending on how one looks at it, it could be considered either appropriate or ironic that in March 1314 the Master of the Templars, James of Molay, was burnt at the stake on an island in the Seine situated not far from Louis's Sainte-Chapelle.

Philip the Fair ordered the arrest of the Templars on suspicion of apostasy, idolatry and sodomy, though the order was never found guilty of these charges; its final dissolution was decreed on the practical grounds that the order's reputation was so damaged that it was no longer capable of carrying out its duties. There has long been a consensus that the charges made in 1307 were false, though historians disagree on the extent to which Philip himself believed them. Two aspects of the trial, however, are incontrovertible. The

30. Archbishop Winchelsey presenting Pope Boniface VIII's Bull 'Clericis Laicos' to Edward I in 1296. Amongst other things, Crusades depended on close co-operation between Church and state for their success.

first is that the final collapse of the Latin establishment in the Holy Land made up an important part of its back-cloth, as the King and his contemporaries sought to make sense of the disaster in traditional terms of human sinfulness. Crudely put, the Templars suffered the fate of scapegoats. Secondly, Philip took the initiative in part because he accepted the role laid down for the French monarchy by his grandfather – purifying the kingdom of heresy in order that it could function as a nursery of Crusaders. Thus the later stage of the trial became entwined with the Crusade plans which Philip pursued towards the end of his reign. Philip was acting in the tradition of St Louis. It is quite possible to imagine Louis taking the same action, though maybe not the same methods, had he been convinced of the Templars' guilt. The difference between the two rulers is that nobody would have questioned Louis's motivation, whereas all too many did that of Philip, viewing him as primarily interested in the Order's famed wealth.

The association of the French monarchy and kingdom with crusading which resulted from St Louis's reign, to which Joinville's text made its contribution, thus conferred decidedly mixed blessings on his successors. On the one hand, they were looked to by most people who hoped to reconquer the Holy Land as the potential leaders of Christendom's combined crusading efforts. This recognition gave them considerable leverage against opposition both at home and abroad, as well as massive financial gains in the form of taxes levied on the Church in France and to some extent elsewhere. From Philip the Fair (1285–1314) through to Philip VI of Valois (1328–50), a series of Crusades were planned in which the precedent of St Louis played a shaping role. On the other hand, as these expeditions all failed to occur, the suspicions voiced about Philip the Fair in relation to the trial of the Templars were echoed more and more frequently. The French kings of the late-thirteenth and early fourteenth centuries experienced a range of financial, political and diplomatic problems, which surpassed anything Louis IX had known. As these problems again and again stood in the way of action, St Louis's glowing example came to resemble the shirt of Nessus, which his successors could neither discard nor wear with ease. Only crushing defeat and sharply reduced expectations brought this period to an end. In 1336, with war against Edward III of England looming, Philip VI secured papal permission to postpone the last, and most ambitious, in this series of projected Crusades. The Italian chronicler Matteo Villani was almost certainly not alone in attributing the series of military disasters suffered by Philip and the French during the early stage of the Hundred Years War to divine punishment for betraying Christ's cause. Joinville might well have agreed with such a judgement.

4

THE 'LIVRE DES FAIS' OF MARSHAL BOUCICAUT:

CRUSADING AND CHIVALRY

In the summer of 1421 Jean II le Meingre, called Boucicaut, Marshal of France, died in Yorkshire, where he was being held prisoner following his capture at the battle of Agincourt. It was appropriate that the fifty-six-year-old Boucicaut should die a long way from his birthplace at Tours, for his life had been characterized by travel, much of it carried out so as to engage in warfare against non-Christians. Such people were generically called 'Saracens' (*Sarrasins*) whether they were Muslims or not, and they were regarded by Boucicaut and his admirers as enemies of the faith. The career of this diminutive, exceptionally bellicose aristocrat serves as a valuable means of understanding how and why crusading survived the disasters of 1291. In particular, the remarkable chivalric biography of Boucicaut, *Le Livre des fais du bon messire Jehan le Maingre* (hereafter *Ldf*), which narrated his life up to 1409, serves, to employ the phraseology of its recent editor Denis Lalande, as 'a grill to decipher history'. For the anonymous author of the *Ldf*, Boucicaut was 'the good champion of Jesus

Christ: in heart, will and deed the just persecutor of the unbelievers'. If anybody was a worthy heir to the crusading legacy of the twelfth and thirteenth centuries, it was Boucicaut.

By any standards Boucicaut's life was full of military activity. He was born in 1366, ten years after France's disastrous defeat at Poitiers, and did not have to wait long to experience combat. At the age of twelve he accompanied the Duke of Bourbon on campaign in Normandy, and he was knighted, aged sixteen, on the eve of the battle of Roosebeke in November 1382. Almost immediately afterwards he began weaving a pattern of far-flung travel which would last for more than two decades. In the early months of 1384 he made his first journey to Prussia to assist the Teutonic Knights in their warfare against the pagan Lithuanians, and he returned to Prussia the following winter. After more campaigns in France's interior, in 1387 Boucicaut accompanied Bourbon to Spain, which had become a theatre of operations in the Anglo-French conflict. There ensued two years of extraordinary travel around the Balkans and the Middle East, at first in the company of his friend Renaud de Roye and later in that of Philip of Artois, Prince of the blood royal and Count of Eu. Hostilities with England had been brought to a temporary halt by the Truce of Leulinghen (1389–92), and this enabled Boucicaut first to distinguish himself at the jousts of Saint-Inglevert in the spring of 1390, and then to undertake a third journey to Prussia in 1390–91. On his return King Charles VI created him Marshal of France on Christmas Day 1391. He won the office on his merits, though it was viewed as appropriate that his father Jean I had been Marshal before him.

Boucicaut's most intensive campaigning against *Sarrasins* took place after he had received the Marshal's baton. In 1396 he was one of the most important participants in the Franco-Hungarian Crusade against the Ottoman Turks, which met with disaster at the battle of Nicopolis (Nikopol), fought on 25 September on the southern shores of the Danube (in present-day Bulgaria). Boucicaut was captured, narrowly escaped execution, and was ransomed. In 1399 he was chosen to lead a French expeditionary force to assist the Byzantine Emperor Manuel II against the Turks. Given his status, experience of the East and military capabilities, he was the King's natural choice as Governor of Genoa, which in 1396 had sought to escape overwhelming domestic and foreign difficulties by placing itself under Charles VI's suzerainty. One of the city's biggest problems was an attempt by King Janus of Cyprus to expel the Genoese from the island's principal port, Famagusta, which they had seized in 1373. The Marshal himself sailed East with a Genoese fleet in 1403 to compel Janus to withdraw his troops. This policing action on Cyprus evolved into a series of raids on the Anatolian and Syrian coasts in the spring and summer. The disruption of trade in the region, in particular the sack of Beirut in August 1403, infuriated the Venetians, and while returning Boucicaut fought a battle against them at Modon, off the Peloponnese. After this the opportunities for fighting *Sarrasins* diminished though the Marshal devised a project for attacking Alexandria in 1407 in which he tried to interest his former enemy King Janus. There was a brief but exhilarating naval skirmish with North African Moors off the coast of Provence in September 1408. The Genoese rebelled against Boucicaut's rule in 1409, depriving him of further access to their fleets and money. Returning to France, he carried out a range of domestic duties in the fraught atmosphere of the Armagnac-Burgundian dispute, before being captured at Agincourt in 1415.

The *Ldf* is our main source for much of what Boucicaut did before 1409, and our only source for some of his campaigns against *Sarrasins*. It has long been hailed as one of the best examples in the late Middle Ages of chivalric biography, a genre in which the protagonist is systematically built up as the embodiment of all knighthood's virtues. In his opening words the author makes clear his high estimation of knighthood: 'By God's will Knighthood (*Chevalerie*) and Wisdom (*Science*) have been placed in the world like two pillars, to uphold the orders of laws both divine and man-made.' They were complementary, for any country lacking wisdom would subside into anarchy while any without knighthood would be conquered by its enemies. It was fitting therefore that the deeds of the finest knights should be celebrated as much as the writings of the great sages. According to its author, the genesis of the work was straightforward. Some of the Marshal's comrades had suggested that it be compiled on the basis of their eye-witness recollections of his activities. These individuals would not be named and the Marshal himself would not be consulted, so the twin charges of flattery and self-aggrandizement could be rebuffed.

We have no idea who wrote the *Ldf*, which has survived in a single manuscript held at the Bibliothèque Nationale in Paris. For some time the suggestion was floated that its author was the prolific Christine de Pisan, but the grounds for this attribution are very thin and we can only place the authorship within the Marshal's circle at Genoa: the biographer finished his text on 9 April 1409, shortly before Boucicaut lost control over the city. For all the coy claims made at the start, Boucicaut probably knew it was being written and it is possible that he even commissioned it. Denis Lalande has described the text as a protracted defence of Boucicaut's controversial actions as

Governor of Genoa, including his brazen appropriation of the city's naval resources for his raids on Muslim ports in 1403, and the hostilities with Venice which ensued. This obviously has a bearing on our use of the *Ldf* to reconstruct crusading attitudes since one would expect a response to such charges to portray the 1403 raids in a highly favourable light. It is certainly true that the Marshal's biographer has an axe to grind, not just in relation to Boucicaut's expedition of 1403 but also in his explanation of the crushing defeat suffered by the Crusaders at Nicopolis. That said, the attitudes on display in the *Ldf* accord very strongly with a large group of chronicles, lives and didactic works written in the late Middle Ages, which celebrated and defended chivalric culture. Among such works were Jean Froissart's Chronicle, Jean Cabaret d'Orville's life of Boucicaut's patron, Louis Duke of Bourbon, Chandos Herald's life of the Black Prince, Gomes Eannes de Zurara's life of Henry 'The Navigator', and Geoffrey of Charny's *Livre de chevalerie*.

The *Ldf* has the weaknesses of most works that set out to champion the cause of a small and rather self-centred élite. In the first place, mistakes which sprang from chivalric notions, including those made at Nicopolis in 1396, are omitted or glossed over. Secondly, the author places the best possible interpretation on Boucicaut's actions; they are shown as rooted in honour, the laudable desire to achieve renown, the love of justice, sympathy for the downtrodden, devotion to God, and loyalty to the King. No reference is made to the pressing needs of career, including good marriage, high office and profit, all of which Boucicaut pursued, with varying degrees of success. This was ironic since Philippe de Mézières, the leading moral commentator on public affairs in France in the late fourteenth century, attributed to Boucicaut's own father Jean the proverb that 'the best fish are found in the sea and the best gifts come from the King'. Thirdly, individuals and groups whose lives were conducted outside the chivalric milieu receive little or no attention. The civilians whose lives were turned outside down by the Marshal's campaigns, the common soldiers who formed a vital part of the armies which he commanded, above all the non-Christians against whom he fought, for the most part are mere bystanders.

These are serious shortcomings but in the case of the *Ldf* they should not be exaggerated. The author did not set out to mislead his readers and when his facts can be checked he proves to be reliable. This is biography, albeit tendentious, and it is historically sound when compared, for example, with the fantasies which Jean Froissart regularly indulged in. The author of the *Ldf* had access to documents written by or for Boucicaut and he included some in their entirety, even though they sometimes muddy or contradict the impression which he is trying to give. On important issues there is more than sufficient evidence available to enable us to avoid the pitfalls which would result from an exclusive dependence on the *Ldf*. And there are some positive things to say in the *Ldf*'s favour. Since the text comes from Marshal Boucicaut's circle, albeit filtered through a writer who was probably better educated than most of its residents, it is a relatively unmediated reflection of that circle's aspirations and behaviour. The author undoubtedly believed that the most worthy exponents of knighthood, not just in France but across the whole of Christendom, would share his hero's keen desire to fight against non-Christians, embracing the *credo* that:

> 'every good Christian and above all every valiant nobleman must desire to work on behalf of the Christian faith, willingly and with good heart helping and upholding each other against the unbelievers'.

Boucicaut went to the Holy Land twice. In 1388–9 he was there as a pilgrim, visiting the church of the Holy Sepulchre and other devotional sites including St Catherine's in Sinai. The Franciscans now had care of the Christian holy places and provided taxes were handed over to the Mamluk authorities pilgrimage was fairly safe. Boucicaut's second visit was very different: it took the form of his raids in August 1403, when he attacked or tried to attack Tripoli, Botron, Beirut, Sidon and finally Latakiah. It probably gave him particular satisfaction to pillage Beirut since he had been detained there for a month when trying to embark for the West in 1389. What he was not able to do was take part in Crusade to recover the Holy Land. As we saw at the close of the previous chapter, the last serious attempt to organize such an expedition was abandoned by Philip VI of Valois in 1336, thirty years before Boucicaut's birth. The Anglo-French war was fatal to any such hopes: a predictable theme running through papal letters in the 1330s and 1340s was that the two monarchies should make peace for the sake of the Holy Land. The disastrous defeats at Crécy (1346) and Poitiers (1356), the appalling loss of life during the Black Death in 1348–9, the economic and social dislocation which followed, and the cession of vast stretches of southern France to England in the Peace of Brétigny in 1360, meant that no French general passage could realistically be planned. No other power tried to take over the mantle of crusading leadership from the French court. Indeed none was able to do so since the Holy Roman empire had entered a prolonged phase of institutional weakness after Frederick II's death in 1250.

The recovery of the Holy Land remained a powerful aspiration; while it did not affect society at large as it had in St Louis's time, it continued to inspire and inflame individuals, and occasionally it resonated through European political and religious life with surprising force. When King Peter I of Cyprus briefly seized Alexandria from the Mamluks in 1365, Peter himself, his chancellor Philippe de Mézières and the papal legate Peter Thomas all portrayed the attack in terms of the old crusading strategy of striking at 'the serpent's head'. In an emotional letter to the Pope and Emperor Peter Thomas echoed Robert of Reims's version of Urban II's Crusade sermon in 1095, calling on them to 'free the holy city of Jerusalem which has been a slave-girl for such a long time. She calls, calls, calls to you, and her cry reaches the ears of the Lord Sabaoth'. There was talk of betrayal when no back-up force appeared and the army withdrew, quite sensibly, to save itself from being wiped out by a Mamluk counter-thrust. In the eyes of contemporaries it was plausible for Peter to cast his campaign in this mould because the kings of Cyprus exercised a legal claim to the kingdom of Jerusalem and were even ceremonially crowned as its rulers following their coronation as kings of Cyprus. Thirty years later some enthusiasts for the Crusade which met its end at Nicopolis nurtured the hope of taking back the holy places once the expedition had achieved its first goal, which was to drive the Turks out of the Balkans. With hindsight this seems naively optimistic, but it fitted a deeply entrenched tendency to set up agendas which brought together very different theatres of operation – one need only think of the Fourth Crusade, or of Louis IX in Tunisia. When he turned down the opportunity to visit Jerusalem as a pilgrim, St Louis expressed his concern that peaceful pilgrimage might supplant the hope of regaining the city's shrines for Christianity through military effort; arguably in the long run it did, but it took a very long time for this to happen.

The fact remained that the absence of large-scale planning made participation in a 'recovery Crusade' impossible. The days of general passages led by European kings had ended with St Louis's death at Carthage in 1270. Men like Boucicaut had to recast their crusading aspirations to fit the changing times. Broadly speaking there were three options open to them: they could take part in what were effectively raids, based on a continuing Latin naval superiority; they could take advantage of larger-scale ventures when these were organized; or they could participate in the campaigns which the Teutonic Knights attempted to launch on a twice-yearly basis against the Lithuanians. One advantage of focusing on Boucicaut is that he made use of all three options in the course of his career, so it is important to establish as clearly as possible the variety of contexts within which he operated.

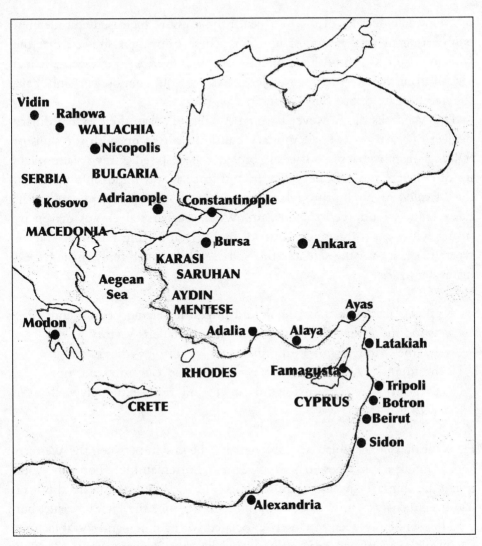

31. The campaigns of Marshal Boucicaut in the eastern Mediterranean.

In the eastern Mediterranean the major factor shaping events was the contraction of Mongol power. For some time after 1291 the Mongol *Ilkhanate* remained a dangerous neighbour for the Mamluks. In 1299 the *Ilkhan* Ghazan crushed a Mamluk army at Homs and seized Damascus; there was excited optimism in the West, but in 1303 the Mamluks defeated their enemies and in 1304 Ghazan died. Gradually relations between the two powers were stabilized and in 1322 peace was made. This was bad news for the Christian kingdom of Armenia, which had relied on the Mongols as a shield against the northward expansion of the Mamluks. The Armenians suffered a number of Mamluk incursions in the late thirteenth century, and in the middle decades of the fourteenth the pressure increased considerably, culminating in total conquest in 1375. These campaigns showed that the Mamluks were as formidable a military power as ever: even if a Crusade had set sail from the West to recover Jerusalem, it would almost certainly have suffered the fate of St Louis's army in Egypt.

The Mamluks did however have an Achilles' heel in their extraordinary neglect of sea power. Their military culture was tied up with the skills of fighting on horseback, and naval combat was despised. Crews were made up of convicts and prisoners of war, and since it was impossible to rise in the Mamluk hierarchy through command at sea, men of talent avoided it. Early failures reinforced this disdain. When Baybars's fleet was driven by strong winds on to reefs off Limassol in 1271, and King Hugh of Cyprus wrote to gloat over the setback, the Sultan in his alleged reply shrugged off his heavy losses:

'It is remarkable that you should prize the seizing of iron and wood more than the seizing of fortified citadels. Victory given by the wind is not beautiful. Only victory by the sword is beautiful... Anyone who is given an oar can row but not everyone who is given a sword can cut and thrust extremely well with it.'

He went on to encapsulate the difference, as he saw it, between the Western and Mamluk approaches to sea power and horsemanship: 'For you, your horses are ships; for us, our ships are horses'. Lack of interest in naval power had been a characteristic of the Muslim regimes since the First Crusade, but it had never before been so closely associated with cultural and social factors.

Given the naval expertise accumulated by the Christian West, Mamluk weakness at sea could only enhance the appeal of raiding on ports which after 1337 extended all the way from Ayas in the gulf of Alexandretta, down through Syria and Palestine, to Alexandria in the western Nile Delta. This was an exceptionally long coastline, and the Latins had long appreciated the advantage which they held over their enemy. In a treatise which he wrote on the recovery of the Holy Land in c.1305, the Master of the Hospitallers Fulk of Villaret advocated a full year of commando-style raids on the Mamluk coastline to prepare the way for the general passage. Fifty or sixty galleys, half of them horse transports, should land in one place after another, destroying and plundering, while the Mamluk forces marched to and fro in vain attempts to meet the threat. By making showy but fake preparations to land and then sailing rapidly to a location four or five days' march away, any attempt by the Mamluks to counter the flotilla's operations would be rendered futile.

> 'In the course of all this coming and going the Saracens' armed forces would exhaust their weaponry and animals, and consume all that they have. (Their civilians) would abandon their settlements, and the agriculture from which most of them get their living. Their condition would degenerate to such an extent that when the (general) passage arrived... it would achieve more than an army three times its size could do, but for the work of this (advance) party.'

Boucicaut's raids in 1403 look remarkably like an attempt to carry out Villaret's prescription. He moved with speed, attacking Tripoli on 6 August, Botron probably on 9 August, Beirut on 10 August, Sidon on 12 August and Latakiah shortly afterwards. But there is no suggestion that he had read Villaret. Rather, his model was Peter of Cyprus's seizure of Alexandria in 1365: the Marshal's goal throughout had been Alexandria, but contrary winds frustrated him both at the start of the campaign and when he had edged his way along the coast as far as Sidon. The allure of capturing Alexandria, as Peter I had done, is easily explained: the sheer bravura of the exploit, as an exhibition of *prouesse*, made it highly tempting to try to repeat it, while Alexandria was far and away the most important port in the Mamluk lands: even if its capture could not be depicted as a first step towards recovering the Holy Land, as it had been in 1365, both the plunder to be won and the serious damage which could be inflicted on the Mamluks made it the goal *sans pareille*. Peter I's campaigns cast a long shadow: in the years following his evacuation of Alexandria the King had raided all the towns which Boucicaut later attacked.

Raiding Mamluk ports was not without its attendant hazards. In the first place, it was bitterly resented by those merchants whose ships were pillaged and trade disrupted. Both in 1365 and in 1403 this meant primarily Venice, which had assiduously built up its commerce with the Mamluk territories. On both occasions the republic hastened to warn the Muslims, and Boucicaut's biographer reported the Marshal's astonishment and fury when he interrogated some Venetians who were apprehended trying to slip out of Beirut after bringing the news. They were lucky to get away with their lives, and although the author of the *Ldf* ascribed Boucicaut's mercy mainly to 'the enormous generosity of his heart, which prevented him making much of it', the Venetians probably owed their escape to Boucicaut's concern not to poison relations between Venice and Genoa. A worse difficulty was the Mamluk reaction to the raids. It was inevitable that if goaded enough they would develop more effective naval power, both to defend their coasts and to carry the war to their enemies' lands, especially Cyprus. King Janus failed to recognize the warning signals, including a raid on Limassol in 1424, to which his response, punitive attacks on the Syrian coast, brought substantial reprisals in 1425 followed by a sea-borne invasion of Cyprus in 1426. What is remarkable is not this belated development of Mamluk sea power, but how long it took to materialize; the Mamluks had been much quicker in getting to grips with siege warfare to reduce Frankish castles and towns in the Holy Land, when they faced the menace of a Mongol attack in the East. It seems that the waning of the Mongol threat played into the hands of men like Peter I, Boucicaut and Janus.

The shrinking of Mongol power also played a key role to the north and north-west of the Mamluk territories: in Anatolia, the Aegean Sea and the region around Constantinople. The arrival of the Mongols in the 1240s had brought chaos to Anatolia, breaking up the Seljuq sultanate, whose origins went back to the time of the First Crusade, and displacing thousands of Turks, who settled in the group of marcher principalities adjoining the Byzantine lands in the west of the peninsula. The *Ilkhanate's* hold over Anatolia was never strong, and by 1300 a number of autonomous Turkish principalities were forming. Those based along Anatolia's western coastline, Karasi, Saruhan, Aydin and Mentese, occupied themselves with eroding the surviving Byzantine lands here. They cultivated an ethos of *jihad*; the bands of warriors perceived themselves as *gazis*, engaged in the expansion of the *Dar-al-Islam* by conquering land and subjugating its Christian inhabitants.

These Turks did not have the good fortune to control the massive resources of the Nile Delta. Even after their principalities became stable, and began to be governed by amirs with courts and hereditary succession, they still needed booty, and to acquire it they had to take to the Aegean Sea and prey on its islands and trading routes. The Byzantine emperors of the Palaeologan dynasty were always hard-pressed financially and at this time they were disbanding their navy, so there were sufficient ship-builders and sailors to meet Turkish needs. This was important: despite what Baybars had claimed in 1271 not everyone could handle an oar. By about 1320 the impact of Turkish raiding was severe enough to register with Venice; the republic's trade in the Aegean was substantial and it still ruled most of the territory which it had acquired at the end of the Fourth Crusade. The other major

Latin power in the region was the Order of St John, or Knights Hospitaller. Following their flight from Acre in 1291 they had successfully relocated their headquarters on the island of Rhodes. Their control over Rhodes was complete by 1310, and while they still hoped to return to the Holy Land, conducting naval operations against the Turks of Anatolia had its own appeal; it would protect the Order's local commerce and its effects could be cited to show that they still had a role in the struggle against Islam, thus justifying their extensive lands and privileges in the West.

The war against *Sarrasins* in this region was thus different from that further south, to the extent that it originated as a response to Muslim aggression, which was itself embedded in a culture of holy war; it was generally reactive rather than proactive, especially on the part of the Venetians, who much preferred diplomacy to fighting. In other respects, however, there was a clear similarity, for here too the war was fought largely at sea, on an intermittent basis, and took the form of sharp skirmishes and raids. For example, in 1334 a flotilla of about forty galleys inflicted a defeat on the ships of Karasi in the gulf of Adramyttion; in 1357 the papal legate Peter Thomas sacked the Turkish fortified town at Lampsakos, opposite Gallipoli; and in the 1360s King Peter I of Cyprus attacked a series of ports along the southern Anatolian coast. This was largely 'hit and run' activity, poorly documented, confused in character and rarely important outside the local or at best regional context. Big armies raised by Crusade preaching and transported eastward in a *passagium* like those led by St Louis would have been redundant in such a conflict, even if circumstances in Europe had favoured their recruitment.

On the other hand, the institutional impact of crusading was felt, because Venice, the Knights Hospitaller and Cyprus were all sophisticated powers and possessed the means to lobby the papal court for the grant of crusading taxes and other revenues on behalf of the war which they were being forced to fight. The popes were normally willing to respond favourably, indeed some of them showed a lively interest in the war in the Aegean. This was partly because it was a way of exerting their authority at a time when it was being increasingly challenged by assertive kings, a very good example of this being the trial of the Templars. But it was also because the popes saw in the war against the Turks a means of sustaining enthusiasm for crusading until political and economic conditions permitted the revival of plans for regaining the Holy Land. Clement VI was very excited by the capture in 1344 of most of the port of Smyrna (Izmir), sanctioning the departure for Smyrna of a sizeable force of Crusaders raised by a French Prince called Humbert of Vienne. The Pope bestowed on Humbert the grandiose title of 'captain of the Apostolic See and leader of the whole army of Christians against the Turks', but he was actually a somewhat ineffectual figure, and when he found out that there was nothing much for him to do at Smyrna he soon left for Rhodes.

By the time Boucicaut reached maturity the situation had changed with the emergence of the Ottoman Turks as the region's dominant power. Their principality originated south of the Sea of Marmora, its first capital being Bursa. They had no outlet to the Aegean Sea, so were not amongst the group of amirates which raided the lands and trading vessels of the Venetians and other westerners. Their Christian opponents were the Byzantines, and it was civil war in the empire which enabled the Ottomans to achieve the crucial step of crossing the Dardanelles into Thrace in the 1340s. When the Marshal was born in 1366 it was apparent that the Ottomans were the most dangerous of the Turkish principalities, and it was largely fear of an attack on Constantinople that drove the Byzantines to reopen negotiations for Church union with the papal court. They persuaded the popes to bring the defence of Constantinople and its Thracian hinterland onto the crusading agenda alongside the protection of the islands and sea-lanes of the Aegean. But if the Byzantines hoped that salvation would come from the West, in a kind of inverted Fourth Crusade, they were disappointed: the papacy itself did not command the resources to provide much assistance and crusading enthusiasm was easily diverted from Constantinople's needs. In particular, Peter of Cyprus's attack on Alexandria in 1365 deprived the Byzantines of men, money and ships. The best that could be achieved was the familiar pattern of raids, the capture of small towns and forts, and intimidating shows of force. In 1366 Amedeo VI Count of Savoy, a cousin of the Emperor John V, led an army of between 3,000 and 4,000 men which took a number of ports including Gallipoli. Amedeo's expedition was quite successful and it formed the clearest precedent for Boucicaut's 'task force' of 1399. The Greeks felt increasingly isolated and the impact of such expeditions on their morale was out of all proportion to their military effect.

The 1370s and 1380s were decades of remarkable conquest for the Ottomans. It was probably in 1369 that they took Adrianople, which became their first European capital. In 1371 they defeated the Serbs at Crnomen and in 1389 they crushed a coalition of Balkan princes at Kosovo, a defeat which came to acquire enormous significance within the national mythology of the Serbs. The Turks conquered Thrace, Macedonia and Bulgaria; Serbia was reduced to vassal status and Wallachia, north of the Danube, paid tribute to the Sultan. In the space of just a few years the Orthodox states of the Balkans, which had served as a useful buffer zone, had effectively disappeared. The Peloponnese and Hungary, lands ruled by Latin Christians, were now directly threatened, initially by the *akinjis*, the Ottoman raiders who still saw themselves as *gazis* expanding the *Dar-al-Islam* by force of arms. The Ottomans were no less successful in Anatolia, where they overran the other Turkish principalities; and they continued to threaten Constantinople, which they held under blockade from 1394 onwards. But for obvious reasons it was the threat to fellow-Catholics in Greece and Hungary that most alarmed the authorities of Europe. Behind Greece was Italy and behind Hungary the Holy Roman empire: the crusading cause was coming home.

In these circumstances of impending crisis tentative plans began to be made for a large-scale Crusade against the Ottomans to drive them out of Europe. The initiative could not be expected to come from the papacy, because in 1378 the Great Schism had broken out in the Church, dividing all of Europe into two obediences owing allegiance to popes who maintained separate courts at Rome and Avignon. Instead, it derived from the French and English courts and from a group of princes, the dukes of Orleans and Burgundy in France and John of Gaunt in England. Following the truce of Leulinghen of 1389 there were hopes on both sides of the Channel that the promotion of a Crusade, which had been impeded for so long by the Anglo-French conflict, could become the vehicle for restoring good relations between the two monarchies. It might exert a similar effect on the Great Schism, restoring unity and peace to the Church. In practice crusading generated rancour and disputes, but the high ideals of the early 1390s reveal that even after three centuries medieval Europe retained its capacity to embark on a major crusading project in a spirit of aspiration.

In practice what made the Nicopolis expedition feasible was less the outpourings of enthusiasts, than the two considerations that had always been prerequisites of crusading: a sustained organizational momentum and the willingness of the fighting elite to participate. The momentum came largely from ducal Burgundy, for in the course of 1395 most of the other high-level interest in the expedition fell away. Duke Philip the Bold, on the other hand, persisted with his plans largely, it would appear, because of the prestige which would accrue to his court. Philip had large if imprecise ambitions for his principality, which included most of the Low Countries as well as Burgundy itself, and he believed that the sponsorship of a Crusade would help promote them. He decided not to go in person, but he placed the financial resources and administrative apparatus of his lands at the disposal of his eldest son John, Count of Nevers. A substantial and well-organized Burgundian contingent was thus guaranteed, giving an assurance to other French magnates who decided to take part that there would actually be an army for them to join. Most of the groups (*montres*) assembled by these magnates departed with Nevers from Montbéliard at the end of April 1396. The expedition had been granted Crusade status by both papal obediences, and by marching overland the army was able to pick up large groups of German and Hungarian Crusaders *en route*. Further east it was also joined by contingents of Wallachians and Transylvanians. As a result of this snowball effect the army which fought at Nicopolis was comparable in size to those of the twelfth and thirteenth centuries: not 100,000 men as used to be suggested, but probably between 10,000 and 20,000.

Although they probably formed no more than a tenth of the force which eventually fought at Nicopolis, the French and Burgundian men-at-arms were its best-equipped soldiers and without them no army would have materialized. Their willingness to take part is striking but we would be wrong to conclude that they were responding to the severity of the Ottoman threat. In the first place, there had been a comparable wave of enthusiasm six years previously when Louis, Duke of Bourbon, responded to a Genoese proposal by leading an expedition of several thousand men against the pirate base of al-Mahdiya in North Africa. The main historian of this campaign, Jean Cabaret d'Orville, wrapped it up in chivalric language very similar to that used in the *Ldf* to describe Nicopolis, and many of those who fought at al-Mahdiya volunteered soon afterwards for the Nicopolis Crusade. Given that the only Christians suffering directly from al-Mahdiya's attentions were traders, it is apparent that it was the opportunity which excited the French, rather than the threat posed by the Muslim enemy. The same probably applied in the case of Nicopolis. This assessment may seem harsh, but it is strengthened by the fact that as late as 1394 Philip the Bold was still weighing the merits of different objectives for his planned expedition. Hindsight allows us to appreciate the full danger posed by the Ottoman Turks, and the velocity of their conquests in the 1370s and 1380s certainly led perceptive contemporaries to express alarm; but we cannot infer from this that there was a general awareness of the situation.

One of the alternative destinations which Duke Philip was still considering in 1394, Prussia, constituted the third theatre for combat against *Sarrasins* during Boucicaut's lifetime. Prussia was one of several off-springs of the synthesis produced during the twelfth and thirteenth centuries of Crusade ideas with German eastward expansion. It was the creation of the Teutonic Knights, brothers of a military order similar to the Hospitaller and Templar, and founded during the Third Crusade. Although primarily dedicated to the defence of the

Holy Land, the Order's overwhelmingly German affiliations made it hard to avoid undertaking commitments also in Eastern Europe and the Baltic region. This was particularly the case when those commitments brought with them the possibility of creating an independent 'order-state', as in Prussia, the land lying on either bank of the Vistula's lower reaches north of Poland. In the early thirteenth century the Poles suffered destructive raids by the pagan Prussians and they responded by appealing to the Teutonic Knights for help. By 1300 the Order had brought Prussia under its control. Given its simultaneous responsibilities in the Latin East, where it held a group of important castles, this would have been impossible without the assistance of armies of Crusaders. Conquest was consolidated by a carefully managed process of settlement that brought thousands of German peasants to Prussia. Most of the 'Old Prussians' came to form a serf class, although their nobles were accorded more generous treatment so as to deprive rebellions of potential leadership.

After 1291 the Teutonic Order was able to focus its attention on Prussia; in 1309 the Knights moved their headquarters from its interim location at Venice to Marienburg (Malbork), an impressive fortress from which they administered their order-state with an unusually high level of efficiency. The main problem now facing the Order came not from arrangements within Prussia but from its eastern neighbour, pagan Lithuania. A *casus belli* existed in the form of Samogitia, the land north of Memel (Klaipeda) which was held by the Lithuanians and coveted by the Knights because it offered land communications between Prussia and their fellow-brethren in Livonia. Some agreement might have been reached over Samogitia, but for the fact that the ruling elites on both sides were by nature bellicose. The Lithuanians were surrounded by powerful enemies: the Knights and Poles in the West, the Russians and Mongols in the East; and their response was the pre-emptive attack, executed with savage efficiency. For their part, the Teutonic Knights were trained to regard pagans as natural enemies; their conquest was not just politically desirable but also the necessary prelude to their conversion. The result was war between the Order and the Lithuanians, which broke out *c.*1300 and lasted for more than a century.

It was natural that the Teutonic Knights would see this war as a continuation of their earlier Crusades against the Prussians. Like those Crusades, it was being waged by a military order against pagans, to defend from attack the christianized lands of Prussia and Livonia, and to bring about the further expansion of Christendom. It was also not surprising, given the Order's limited military resources, that it would as before do all in its power to encourage and welcome volunteers from the West to help it sustain the war effort. The Order did not create the war for the sake of an image of unceasing hostility towards paganism, but this image did make it possible to drive the war forward and it was therefore assiduously promoted. Unquestionably it enjoyed great success, for over the course of the century many thousands of volunteers came to take part in the conflict. At first sight this is surprising. The Order provided hospitality before and after the campaigns, but the campaigning itself was for the most part both tedious and physically taxing. There were about 100 miles of marsh and dense forest between Lithuania and Prussia, so a good deal of each volunteer's time was spent actually reaching the enemy, hence the German name *Reise* (journey) given to each campaign. This inhospitable terrain placed severe constraints on the timing of hostilities, for they could only take place when weeks of hot sun or hard winter frosts had made the roads negotiable. Even when the enemy came within reach, combat as often as not took the form of skirmishes or destructive raids on villages, a pattern not dissimilar to that of the fighting which was taking place in the eastern Mediterranean.

Viewed from a different perspective, however, the attractiveness of the *Reisen* to anybody harbouring a desire to fight *Sarrasins* does become apparent. In the first place, they were regular in character. An expedition like that to Nicopolis was wholly exceptional, and even raids on Muslim ports in the Mediterranean, in Anatolia, Syria, Egypt or the Maghrib, were adventitious. Prussia was distant but it could be reached without serious difficulty and nobles going there knew exactly what they could expect once they reached Königsberg (Kaliningrad) – the customary assembly point. The Teutonic Order's patroness was the Virgin Mary, and the Knights would attempt to launch a *Winterreise* on or around the feast of her Purification on 2 February, and a *Sommerreise* at the time of her Assumption on 15 August. Every effort would be made to organize at least a nominal *Reise*, though sometimes the adverse weather conditions caused delays. The grim terrain, harsh climate, and long march may well have added to the appeal of an exercise which was intended to be a test of endurance. Geoffrey of Charny had commented baldly that men-at-arms in search of honour just put up with the cold when it was cold and with the heat when it was hot; 'everything feels good to them because of the great pleasure they derive from winning honour and living honourably'.

As for the brutal and shabby nature of much of the fighting, both fighting men and their apologists were well used to glamourizing such unpromising material. This point requires emphasis because it is crucially important for understanding the approach which Boucicaut's contemporaries had not just towards the *Reisen* but towards all combat against *Sarrasins*. Reading the accounts given of individual *Reisen* by Wigand of Marburg, the Order's herald, one is constantly struck by the contrast between the squalid massacres perpetrated during the *Reisen* and the language of chivalry deployed by Wigand. It is tempting to ascribe it to hypocrisy on the part of the Order and its volunteers, or to use the language of camouflage and disguise, which implies self-deception; certainly it is hard to grasp the thought-world of men for whom such reality and rhetoric could co-exist. But there are ways to enter that world. One is to share with contemporaries the knowledge that pitched battles on any scale were rare events. A good reason for going on a *Reise* was to be dubbed, since it was considered particularly meritorious to undergo that ceremony after an encounter with *Sarrasins*. But it was unrealistic to expect to be dubbed after a battle; one might have to settle for a skirmish at a river crossing, or the smoking ruins of a village bathhouse. Expectations changed to fit circumstances. It is also important to appreciate that even in warfare between Christians in Western Europe it was only gradually becoming accepted that the lives and goods of non-combatants should be spared. Many of the English knights who took part in *Reisen* had been on *chevauchées* (large-scale raids) in France in which comparable atrocities had been committed; early in 1360, for example, Edward III's army pillaged and burned its way through Champagne after the King's failure to take Reims. Nobody would claim that Lithuanian pagans had more rights than French peasants.

The popularity of the *Reisen,* and the enthusiasm which greeted recruitment for the expeditions to al-Mahdiya and Nicopolis, are enough to show that Boucicaut was far from exceptional in being immensely attracted by what one chronicler described as 'front-lines in the struggle against the pagans' (*frontes guerrarum paganorum*). There was clearly a consensus of agreement with Philippe de Mézières's remark that 'the first and principal glory of the dignity of true chivalry is to fight for the faith'. Where Boucicaut was unusual was in the variety of his experience. Even in this respect he was not unique. John Holland, Earl of Huntingdon and half-brother of Richard II, displayed a similar range of interests between 1386 and 1397. But the closest parallel is probably a fictional character, Chaucer's Knight in *The Canterbury Tales*. Chaucer depicted his Knight as a paragon of chivalry, and in his 'Prologue' he presented a list of the places where the Knight had fought in defence of the faith. Writing in *c*.1384, Chaucer could not include Nicopolis, as he surely would have done had he written after that Crusade. His Knight's service did, however, include both sea-borne raids on Muslim ports and participation in the *Reisen*. Chaucer shows that the latter had even given rise to an English verb ('he reysed'), and he portrays the Knight being seated at the Teutonic Order's Table of Honour (*Ehrentisch*), the place reserved at their feasts for their most honoured guests. The Knight had also taken part in Peter of Cyprus's capture of Alexandria in 1365 and in his earlier raids on Adalia (Satalia) and Alaya. Like Boucicaut he had travelled in a non-combatant capacity, for Chaucer depicted him jousting at Tlemcen in North Africa. He had also fought at one 'front-line' which was no longer available in Boucicaut's time, for he campaigned with Alfonso XI of Castile at the siege of Algeciras, a port in Granada, in 1344. Six years after taking Algeciras Alfonso XI died during the Black Death and Castilian operations against Granada ground to a halt, not to revive for many years.

These thirty or so lines in Chaucer's 'Prologue' have been subjected to a vast amount of commentary and there is no doubt that, interpreted with proper care, they have a lot to tell us about warfare against the *Sarrasins* in the time of Chaucer and Boucicaut. It is fruitless to search for an English knight who might have served as a model for Chaucer since that gains nothing and shows scant respect for the poet's imagination. We can however say that based just on Boucicaut's own experiences, the eclectic career enjoyed by Chaucer's Knight becomes perfectly viable: had he been sixteen at Algeciras, as Boucicaut was when dubbed before Roosebeke, then he would have been in his mid-fifties at the time of his Canterbury pilgrimage. Chaucer wrote of his Knight that 'from the moment that he first began to ride about the world, he loved chivalry, truth, honour, freedom and all courtesy', phrases for which one could easily find parallels in the *Ldf*. The Knight's remarkable skill on the tournament field and in the jousting lists reflected the renown that Boucicaut earned jousting at Saint-Inglevert in 1390. At one point the parallel with Boucicaut is especially revealing. In lines 64–66 Chaucer says that the Knight fought for the Turkish amir of Balat (Palatye) 'against another heathen in Turkey'. It is an activity which has struck some commentators as incongruous, to the extent that this supposed hero of the faith was fighting for Christ's enemies. But in 1388 Boucicaut and Renaud de Roye offered their services to Sultan Murad I 'if he should make war against any Saracens', an incident which Boucicaut's biographer, like Chaucer, clearly thought to reflect well on his subject. There is no suggestion that either Boucicaut or Chaucer's Knight contemplated fighting for Muslims against Christians, which would indeed have been dishonourable in the extreme; but fighting for heathens with conspicuous skill and courage at the same time as displaying Christian devotion was meritorious. It might even have been regarded as a roundabout way of converting them.

Turning now to Boucicaut's own career, what strikes one first about his three *Reisen* of 1384–5 and 1390–1 is his good fortune. The Marshal's biographer makes no claim that Boucicaut was anything but conventional in his attitude towards Prussia. He went there early in 1384, once a truce had been sealed between England and France, 'as is common practice amongst those who desire to travel in order to grow their reputations'. His return to Prussia at the end of the same year derived from rumours that 'there would be a really good *Reise* (*belle rese*) this season'. His third *Reise*, in 1390–1, was a sort of substitute for going on the Duke of Bourbon's al-Mahdiya expedition; the King had refused to let him accompany his patron's army and Boucicaut got so irritated that he did not want to stay at court, so he decided to go to Prussia. He was lucky because he was catching the last phase in the popularity of the *Reisen*. Grand Duke Jogailo of Lithuania was baptized early in 1386 in association with a dynastic union between his state and Poland, and the conversion of the Lithuanians was set in motion. For years to come the Teutonic Knights argued that this whole conversion process was a sham and that the war must continue, but by the end of the century their argument was wearing thin. In 1410 the Knights suffered a disastrous defeat at the hands of the Poles and Lithuanians at Tannenberg (Grünwald) and their order-state in Prussia entered a long period of decline.

But if the *Reisen* had already entered their Indian Summer when Boucicaut was in Prussia, it was a particularly splendid one. His first two *Reisen* took place during the winter when operations were normally limited in scope, and there was no *Reise* at all in the winter of 1390–1 because the weather was too mild, but by waiting until the summer of 1391 Boucicaut was able to experience a campaign of unusual splendour. There was a large concentration of volunteers including several hundred men-at-arms from Meissen led by their Margrave Frederick IV. The new Grand-master, Conrad of Wallenrode, decided to seize the opportunity by taking the field in person. Boucicaut was so impressed that 'he raised his banner for the first time', which seems to have meant that he accorded the enterprise the status of a full-scale campaign rather than a raid. Several Lithuanian strongholds were stormed and a new fortress called Ritterswerder ('le Chastel des Chevaliers') was constructed.

The image behind the *Reisen*, to which Boucicaut and his biographer subscribed, was essentially the same as that which inspired the proponents of the Nicopolis Crusade: Christendom's knights fighting side-by-side in brotherly harmony against pagans. By 1391 that image was beginning to dissolve as the 'pagans' were being converted. A few years previously the crusading enthusiast Philippe de Mézières had welcomed this, bringing the

32. Naval warfare in the thirteenth century. The methods of assault shown in this illumination from Matthew Paris's *Chronica Majora* may seem clumsy and unsophisticated, but the superiority of the Latin West over the Muslims in the techniques of seaborne combat played a vital role throughout the Crusades. It helped compensate for the overwhelming numerical advantage which the Muslims enjoyed.

Lithuanians into his grand plan for a recovery Crusade that would operate on several fronts. And the image was flawed in another respect, because for all the efforts made by the Teutonic Knights to foster chivalric concord on the 'Christian' side of the religious divide, Europe's animosities could not be excluded. At the time Boucicaut fought volunteers belonged to opposing obediences in the Great Schism; perhaps of even more importance was the fact that they had fought on different sides in the Hundred Years War. The effects were demonstrated clearly in 1391 by the 'Douglas affair'. Sir William Douglas was a Scots knight who was killed by some English volunteers in a brawl at Königsberg. According to one account they rather un-chivalrously took advantage of Douglas getting his leg caught in a hole. Boucicaut ostentatiously challenged Douglas' unknown murderer to single combat, but the

English closed ranks and refused the challenge; they would take on any Scots knight who came forward, but not Boucicaut, whose reputation they were well aware of. The diplomacy of the Anglo-French conflict had been transplanted to Königsberg, and the atmosphere was so poisoned by the incident that the customary Table of Honour had to be postponed. Somewhat bizarrely, it was held on the campaign itself, where the volunteers ate and drank wearing full armour, presumably for fear of Lithuanian attack.

Although Boucicaut's third *Reise* originated in his annoyance with the King for refusing to allow him to accompany Bourbon's expedition to Tunisia, relations between the two men must have been fundamentally sound, for immediately on his return from Prussia Boucicaut was appointed Marshal of France. It was this post which lay behind Boucicaut's ability to initiate even small-scale operations against the Turks and Mamluks in the eastern Mediterranean between 1399 and 1403, first in his capacity as commander of Charles VI's 'task force' to Constantinople and then as Governor of Genoa. As in Prussia, fortune favoured Boucicaut. His responsibilities accorded with his personal inclinations, and they gave him the resources, in men, money and ships, to wage war on the *Sarrasins*. In 1399, an urgent plea from the Byzantine Emperor Manuel II for assistance to break the Ottoman blockade of Constantinople triggered Charles VI's decision to send his Marshal at the head of about 2,000 men. He led a series of daring raids on Turkish forts and towns in the vicinity of Constantinople, which had the effect of opening up, for a time, the city's supply routes. He agreed to accompany Manuel back to France to plea for more help so that the gains made by his expedition would not prove short-lived. And he made provision for a force of 100 men-at-arms, 100 esquires and a contingent of crossbowmen, commanded by Jean de Châteaumorand, to remain at Constantinople to bolster Greek morale during Manuel's absence. Sufficient money was left for their payment and food, and the Genoese and Venetians agreed to provide some naval support for the French garrison.

Boucicaut's expedition to Constantinople presented the Marshal with a relatively clear-cut strategic scenario, which brought out the best in him as a commander. Moreover, there is no trace in the *Ldf* or other sources of his harbouring anti-Orthodox sentiments of the type voiced by some of his contemporaries, including Philippe de Mézières. The Marshal appears to have felt genuine sympathy for the plight of his fellow-Christians in the East and to have committed himself to lobbying on their behalf. His military operations, and in particular the garrison which he installed before departure, bear a strong similarity to Louis IX's activities in the Holy Land after the failure of his

Egyptian campaign. He was doing what he could to further a genuine rapprochement between Latin and Orthodox Christianity on the basis of interests which the Ottomans had brought firmly together. But the weakness of the French and English monarchies at this point stood in the way of Emperor Manuel II taking further what Boucicaut had achieved. Charles VI's periodic fits of madness were paralyzing royal policy in France and Henry IV's hold on the throne in England was too tenuous for him to help the Greeks. Manuel II returned home in 1402 empty-handed. Châteaumorand did what he could to stave off a renewal of Ottoman pressure on Constantinople but by 1402 the city was again facing famine. It was the devastating defeat inflicted on the Ottomans at Ankara by the Mongol war-lord Tamerlane, on 28 July 1402, which coincidentally released Constantinople from the Turkish blockade and had the effect of giving the shrunken Byzantine empire its final fifty years of life.

A case can therefore be constructed for Boucicaut's activities in the region of Constantinople being both sensible and enlightened, almost an attempt to establish a French protectorate there resembling that set up by St Louis in the 1250s at Acre. It is less easy to build a similar case for his raids on the Anatolian and Mamluk ports in 1403. It is true that after the battle of Ankara Boucicaut, now Governor of Genoa, persuaded the Genoese to attack Muslim shipping so fiercely that the city and the sultanate were in a state of undeclared war when Boucicaut arrived at Rhodes in June 1403. The same did not, however, apply to the Anatolian port of Alaya (Scandelore), which he attacked before his series of raids on Mamluk targets. If we accept the account given by the Marshal's biographer, the Alaya raid was undertaken in a remarkably thoughtless manner. While on Rhodes, awaiting the return of the Grand-master from a peace-making mission to King Janus of Cyprus, Boucicaut enquired of the Hospitallers and Genoese 'where it seemed most convenient to carry out a raid (une rese) on the enemies of the faith'. They recommended Alaya, partly because it would serve as a useful base if Janus proved stubborn and an invasion of Cyprus was called for. The amir of Alanya was astonished by the aggression which resulted: 'he was amazed that (Boucicaut) was attacking him so violently, given the fact that he had never inflicted harm on him or on his people, or indeed on the Genoese, which could explain this behaviour'. Peace was made and the Marshal embarked his troops.

At this point Boucicaut was informed that Janus had come to terms and no campaign in Cyprus would be necessary. It was possible to focus on the war against the Mamluks, and there ensued the series of raids on Tripoli, Botron, Beirut, Sidon and Latakiah, as the Marshal vainly pursued his goal of an assault on the prize target of Alexandria. Given the costs attached to these in terms of Venetian hostility and Mamluk reprisals, it is difficult to rebut the charge that Boucicaut was acting irresponsibly and selfishly. The only alternative is to argue that he viewed the damage inflicted on the Ottoman state at the battle of Ankara as effectively terminal, removing the threat which they had posed and making it possible once again to concentrate on attacking the Mamluks in preparation for the longed-for recovery of the Holy Land. Such an argument, however, receives very little support from the *Ldf*: in his description of the raids the Marshal's biographer mentions neither Tamerlane's successes nor the recovery of the Holy Land. The series of attacks are cast in the same light as the Alaya raid and indeed the *Reisen*: 'his praiseworthy desire to do harm to the unbelievers'. It is true that the 1407 proposal to attack Alexandria is related to the loss of 'the noble lands beyond the sea, which by right form the inheritance of the Christians', but the reference is very general and the goal of the adventure is depicted in the usual general way as 'great honour for the conquerors and maximum gain for the whole of Christendom'.

It is not the job of the historian to award prizes for common sense or foresight. On the other hand, it is legitimate to enquire whether Boucicaut was acting in accordance with essential strategic considerations. And setting aside the argument about Tamerlane and Ankara, it is hard to see how he could have been doing so. The 'smash and grab' mentality lying behind his raids seems to have possessed no firmer underpinning than the idea that destruction inflicted on the *Sarrasins* was by definition a good thing. Awakening the sleeping dragon of Mamluk naval power was not considered. For that matter, the Marshal appears to have been unconcerned about the way in which his espousal of Genoese interests was undermining the Lusignan monarchy in Cyprus and thereby weakening a power which for more than century had acted as a Christian front-line state. He was aware of the argument that Cyprus constituted a valuable springboard for Christian armies in the East, as for example in St Louis's Egyptian campaign, but was quite happy to turn it upside down by casting Alaya in the role of a jumping-off point for an invasion of Cyprus.

What is striking is that this apparent lack of reflection and foresight co-existed with a good eye for precision when it was called for. The letter which Boucicaut wrote or commissioned defending his position *vis-à-vis* Venetian claims of aggression is a carefully constructed legal argument, and in 1407 the Marshal produced detailed costings for a proposed attack on Alexandria which he hoped would make it financially viable. His biographer was not wildly exaggerating when he claimed that:

'Whenever he goes to war, he carefully weighs up the pros and cons, whether he has just cause, what the outcome will be, what resources he has in men and money, what his enemy's strength is, the condition of the land and the battleground, the season and the weather, in fact everything that could either harm or help him, reflecting with good sense on all of it.'

Naturally any judgement on Boucicaut's approach towards the conduct of warfare against the *Sarrasins* must hinge to a large degree on the Nicopolis expedition: this was his grand opportunity, a campaign on a scale not experienced by any other generation since 1270. The Crusade's overall significance resists confident assessment. A Christian victory might have brought about the expulsion of the Ottoman Turks from their European provinces, given that Tamerlane's arrival a few years later would have prevented them drawing on reserves from Anatolia. By contrast, defeat at Nicopolis reduced the West to such limited measures as Boucicaut's own task force of 1399. The problem is that the scale and consequences of the battle of Ankara overshadow Nicopolis, not least in the Ottoman sources, in which Bayezid's victory in 1396 scarcely registers when compared with the tidal wave of destruction which arrived six years later. Nor is it easy to draw up a balanced view of the impact of Nicopolis in the West, because political circumstances in France and England changed so radically in the last years of the century, with Charles VI's escalating bouts of madness and Richard II's downfall. That said, Nicopolis does have a claim to be considered as the last major international Crusade, in which an army recruited from a number of European countries set out to combat the Muslims in the East. This makes it the more tempting to compare the motivation and approach of its participants with those of earlier Crusaders.

The author of the *Ldf* is ill-informed on the expedition's origins, seeing it as the response by Philip Count of Eu to a plea from King Sigismund of Hungary for help against an impending Turkish attack. The Burgundian diplomatic background, which we know was crucially important, is totally ignored; in fact Boucicaut plays a more significant role than Philip the Bold, with Sigismund specifically requesting the Marshal's assistance. We could dismiss this as *amour propre* on Boucicaut's part, were it not for the fact that he had visited the Hungarian court in 1388. The King's personal approach to Boucicaut was thus at least feasible, and of the three reasons which are given for Boucicaut's enthusiastic response, one is his gratitude to Sigismund. The second is Boucicaut's fondness for Philip of Eu and the third, we are not at all surprised to hear, 'that he wanted more than anything else to fight in a battle against Saracens'. Turning to John of Nevers, the Marshal's biographer relates his keenness directly to his youth and status:

> 'He was then in the full flower of youth, and wanted to follow the path sought by the virtuous, that is to say, the honour of knighthood. He considered that he could not use his time better than in dedicating his youth to God's service, by bodily labour for the spreading of the faith, and desired greatly to take part in this honourable venture.'

There was a truce with England; France's young knights were bored and the enterprise itself was honourable.

The author of the *Ldf* provided the names of the expedition's key figures: John of Nevers, Philip of Eu, Henry and Philip of Bar, and Jacques Count of La Marche, all five royal kinsmen. Boucicaut's name occurs only in the next tier, that of the barons, but he was still an important participant. This was partly because of his expertise and reputation, and partly because the *montre* which he led, and paid for himself, comprised the sizeable force of seventy men-at-arms; fully in accordance with previous Crusades, fifteen were his own kinsmen. Although not a member of the council set up by Philip the Bold to give his son advice, Boucicaut was listed among those whom Nevers was to consult 'when it seems appropriate'. Coincidentally both the Marshal and the Constable, Philip of Eu, were members of the Crusade, but neither exercised their office: it must be stressed that this was not a royal army like those of St Louis, but a composite venture much more like the First or Fourth Crusades. We know little about the frame of mind of participants from Germany and Hungary, but the sources for the French and Burgundian contingents agree with the *Ldf* that they served above all for chivalric reasons: to display their *prouesse* in the most elevated theatre of operations which they could imagine, that of warfare against *Sarrasins*. For squires in particular it was a golden opportunity, and at the first engagement at Vidin there seems to have been a mass dubbing, including Nevers and the Count of La Marche. To that extent the expedition was comparable to the summer *Reisen,* and Philip the Bold's uncertainty about whether to direct his expedition to Prussia or to Hungary becomes more comprehensible.

No Crusade was ever fought in a purely selfless frame of mind, if by that we mean that the participants waged war without thinking about acquiring land, booty, relics or glory. This will be clear from previous chapters. But there are grounds for arguing that in the case of the Nicopolis expedition the obsession with displaying *prouesse* on an individual basis played a key role in bringing about disaster. This can only be said tentatively because the sources are an interpretative minefield. Ever since the Second Crusade, failure in God's cause had been accounted for in terms of the licentious behaviour of Crusaders, their abandonment by God on the grounds that they were unworthy to be his agents. This theme of *peccatis exigentibus* runs through several of the most important accounts of the Nicopolis campaign, above all that by the 'Religious of St Denis', the monk at the royal abbey of St Denis who acted as semi-official chronicler for the French court. This account portrays the French as feckless in the extreme, gambling, whoring, drunken and vainglorious wastrels who more or less invited disaster to descend on their heads. The situation is further complicated by the existence of a French domestic context for the debate about why the Crusade failed: for some, it strengthened the impression created by the defeats suffered at the hands of the English that the country's military aristocracy was in urgent need of reform.

In his account of the campaign, the Marshal's biographer makes it clear that he intends to engage with these criticisms and to set the record straight. A key accusation was that the French, including the Burgundians, were undisciplined, and that when they clashed with the Turks their formations were chaotic; small groups engaged the enemy with no co-ordination and were massacred as a result. On the contrary, the author of the *Ldf* claimed that the French had ample time 'to place themselves in very good order, which they did as well as the situation demanded'. Defeat ensued not through the fault of the French, but because of the treachery of the Hungarians, most of whom deserted their allies, and the overwhelming numbers of the Turks. Fortune was against the French, but they more than lived up to their reputation for courage and ardour, 'no people has ever existed in the world who have proved themselves to be bolder or better fighters, more steadfast or more knightly, than the French'.

It might be supposed that the *Ldf* loses its value as a source when dealing with 'le voyage de Honguerie', as contemporaries called the Nicopolis Crusade, because of its author's concern to defend the reputation of the Marshal and his fellow-combatants. It is true that his formulaic descriptions of Boucicaut and the other leaders fighting like heroes against Sultan Bayezid's hordes have to be discounted. But his concern to depict the expedition in the best possible light has its uses, for one can assume that the author sees nothing wrong in events which to us support the charge that the Crusaders brought about their own failure. One good example occurred during the march along the Danube, when Boucicaut and Philip of Eu

33. Carved capital with fighting knights, San Marcello Maggiore, Apulia.

learned that the army's next objective was the town of Rachowa. Together with several other leaders, the two men rode through the night so as to be the first to reach Rachowa. There they plunged straight into action. It was a bravura act of *prouesse* but it could easily have led to many of the expedition's commanders being massacred or captured. Military ordinances in this period, such as those set down for the English royal army at Durham in 1385, were beginning to forbid such potentially disastrous initiatives. At al-Mahdiya in 1390 the Duke of Bourbon had rebuked Boucicaut's younger brother Geoffrey for challenging the *Sarrasins* without first securing his permission. The irony was that in the French royal army breaches of discipline of this kind would have been punished by the Marshal and Constable: the very men who in this instance were responsible for it.

The same subordination of military logic to chivalric initiative lay behind the central error that was committed at the battle of Nicopolis, the initial charge by the French volunteers. King Sigismund knew that it made good sense to keep this superb force of cavalry in reserve and to wear down the Turks with his infantry first. But this was anathema to the French on several grounds. Being in the vanguard was a point of honour in the chivalric code. It was prescribed in the instructions which Philip the Bold drew up for John of Nevers: 'My lord the Count and his company are to request that they form the vanguard'. In other respects these instructions were sensible, but the Duke was paying the heavy costs of his son's participation and it is understandable that he regarded it as inappropriate that a contingent as well-equipped and splendid as that led by his son should not be at the front of the attack. There was the additional problem that the French response to the devastating impact of English arrows on their cavalry charges had been their effective abandonment of such charges since the battle of Poitiers. A major feature of the Crusade's attraction to the French nobility was not just that they would have the chance to take part in a battle against *Sarrasins,* but that it would enable them to take part in a mounted charge, something denied them for a generation. The difficulty was that this approach did not take into account Turkish battlefield tactics, with which King Sigismund seems to have become familiar. Their best troops, the mounted *sipahis* and the janissary infantry, were rarely committed to the front line, which was assigned to their lightly armed *akinji* cavalry. Charging uphill, the French dispersed the *akinjis* without serious difficulty, but they were held up by rows of sharpened stakes which had been driven into the ground, and defeated by the Sultan's reserves, which he had kept concealed beyond the hill's summit. Cut off from their allies, they were all killed or taken prisoner.

Reconstructing the battle in greater detail than this becomes problematic. It is probable that the Wallachians and Transylvanians did desert: from the start they were half-hearted in their support for the Crusade and there was no reason for them to throw their lives away for a cause which must have appeared hopeless. The charge is less likely to be true in the case of the Hungarians; even the author of the *Ldf* admits that some of them stood by their French allies. It is difficult to deny that the French made a considerable contribution to their own defeat even if one sets to one side the wilder accusations of indiscipline and miscalculation made in some of the sources. The fact was that attitudes which taken in isolation were perfectly laudable, including courage, audacity and the desire to excel, became catastrophic in these circumstances. This was not of course unprecedented: one need only think of Robert of Artois's rashness in charging into Mansurah in 1250. Nor was such behaviour by any means limited to warfare against *Sarrasins.* At the battle of Agincourt similar traits would recur, including the insistence of all the French commanders that they fight in the first line of battle. Contemporaries recognized a trend: criticizing the contempt displayed during the Agincourt campaign towards commoners who were fighting for the King, Jean Juvenal des Ursins compared it with what had happened at Courtrai, Poitiers and Nicopolis. Nonetheless, there are grounds for believing that the strong association of crusading in this period with the demonstration of chivalric *prouesse* was especially detrimental to military efficiency. As one of the expedition's most experienced and respected commanders, it was up to Boucicaut to counterbalance this with sane counsel, and he failed to do so. The only thing that might have saved 'le voyage de Honguerie' was a field commander with the energy and skills of Bohemond of Taranto, Boniface of Montferrat or Richard Coeur de Lion. Instead there was a leadership vacuum which allowed the expedition's structural and cultural deficiencies to come to the fore, bringing about disaster.

The dominance of chivalric aspirations on the Nicopolis Crusade was accompanied by the disappearance of penitential rites and behaviour. So far as one can see, little remained of the elaborate ceremonies of pilgrimage, which had been so characteristic of preparations for crusading in the age of St Louis and Joinville. Though Boucicaut's biographer stressed the Marshal's custom of undertaking pilgrimages before major undertakings, he mentioned none in his account of Nicopolis. Only in his description of the battle's aftermath, when Bayezid ordered the massacre of the majority of his prisoners, does the author of the *Ldf* abruptly change his tone, writing with some feeling of their deaths as martyrs for the faith:

'This death was hard to bear and the situation pitiable in the extreme. Nonetheless, good Christians must believe that they were happy and fortunate to perish in this way; because we all have to die, and God granted that they should suffer the most holy and worthy death available to a Christian. According to our beliefs, their death exalted the Christian faith, and it placed them in the company of the blessed martyrs who form the most favoured of all the orders of saints in paradise. There is no doubt that if they died in a state of grace, which God permit, then they are saints in paradise.'

Boucicaut himself narrowly escaped death. He was saved by quick thinking on the part of Nevers, who indicated to the Sultan by crossing two fingers that Boucicaut was as dear to him as a brother; it was therefore worth keeping him alive to be ransomed. Boucicaut's biographer commented that the Marshal was saved by God to avenge on the *Sarrasins* 'the death of this glorious company'. This was a somewhat grandiloquent view, though the exaction of revenge does seem to have entered into his motivations after 1396.

In one document included within the text of the *Ldf*, Boucicaut himself reflected on the attractions of warfare against the *Sarrasins*. The document was his proposal for an assault on Alexandria, which the Marshal entrusted to his envoys in August 1407 for communication to King Janus of Cyprus. While there is no reason to doubt that Boucicaut's biographer presented an accurate version of the Marshal's attitudes, it is obviously useful to have this unmediated evidence of his outlook. Boucicaut stated that he was ready to commit his own person and goods to the expedition, as well as those of his kinsmen, friends and household. This readiness sprang from four reasons:

> 'The first is pure love for our Saviour, the desire to serve him, for the benefit and exaltation of Christendom. The second, to acquire merit for our soul. The third, so that we may be instrumental in [King Janus] using his strength and his youth [sic: Janus was actually more than thirty years old] for good purposes, which will earn him praise for all time. And the fourth reason is the one which should move every knight and gentleman to employ his body unceasingly in the pursuit of arms, the earning of honour and renown'.

It is significant that two of these four reasons relate to religious ideas. It is often argued that most of the devotional content of crusading had been drained away by this point, so it is interesting that in Boucicaut's perception it continued to be important, not only in terms of the benefits which Christendom would derive from it, but also from the viewpoint of the Marshal's own hopes of salvation. What is striking about both aspects is, however, that the frame of reference has become generalized. The traditional justifications of crusading, notably the defence or recovery of Christian lands and communities, are still referred to; at least as frequent, however, are sweeping and vague comments on damage being inflicted on the unbelievers, the 'exaltation' or spread of Christendom, or service to Christ and Christendom. The explanation given for the raids of 1403 is typical: 'the good of Christendom, the exaltation and spread of the faith, and the confusion and ruin of the Saracens.' This of course is to be expected given the range of Boucicaut's activities, his generic application of the word 'Saracen' to Turks, Arabs and Lithuanians alike, and the lack of consideration which he appears to have given to strategic thinking.

This diffusion of warfare against the *Sarrasins* was complemented by the fragmentation of crusading's central features. It is not documented in the *Ldf* that Boucicaut ever took the Cross, made a Crusader's vow, or formally received the Crusader's indulgence. He certainly had opportunities to do all three, especially during the Nicopolis Crusade. If he chose not to, it was presumably because he was confident that his soul would benefit in a less formal sense, through God's recognition of his services. He almost certainly agreed with Geoffrey of Charny's claim in *Le Livre de chevalerie* (*c.*1350) that:

> '...anyone who makes war against the enemies of the faith, and to
> sustain Christendom and maintain the faith of Our Lord, engages
> in a war which is righteous, holy, sure and secure; his body will
> be honoured in a saintly fashion and his soul will be carried swiftly
> to paradise, in holiness and without the pain (of purgatory)'.

This being the case, the canonistic mechanisms of Crusade were perhaps considered to be dispensable. Making the vow entailed burdensome legal obligations which many people disliked; in the early fourteenth century some people who took the Cross made conditional vows incorporating escape clauses. And in Boucicaut's lifetime it became unnecessary to make vows to secure the Crusader's spiritual rewards, for during the Great Schism (1378–1417) plenary indulgences could be obtained much more easily than had once been the case; both papal obediences, financially hard-pressed, made them available in exchange for cash payments.

We should not deduce from this that Boucicaut lacked conventional devotion. Prayer, fasting, charity and pilgrimage all feature in the *Ldf* and other contemporary descriptions of the Marshal; he made some donations to religious houses and in 1406 he founded a hospital. But the penitential aspect of crusading had been marginalised by the emphasis that increasingly had been placed, since Pope Innocent III's time, on the rewarding of military service. Over the course of time this emphasis became fused with the pursuit of chivalric honour and renown (the Marshal's fourth reason), and it was hard for these to co-exist with the self-abasement which was integral to the practice of pilgrimage. The two were bound to become uncoupled, above all during the Nicopolis Crusade, when the showcasing of Burgundian wealth made the discrepancy between them particularly jarring to contemporaries like the Religious of St Denis. As if to compensate for the evaporation of this religious ethos, features of traditional crusading which were more compatible with chivalric aspirations, above all conspicuous veneration of the saints, became more conspicuous. Above all, this applied to the cults of St George and the Virgin. In no respect was Boucicaut more typical of his age than in his veneration for the Virgin, whose intercession he thanked for his escape from death in 1396. Her banner always played a large role on the *Reisen* and Boucicaut's biographer is careful to specify who carried it during all of his major ventures. At Nicopolis John of Nevers decreed that it be carried by John of Vienne, Admiral of France, 'because he was the most valiant and most experienced amongst them', while in 1399 Boucicaut assigned it to Pierre de Grassay, 'because he had the most experience and was a valiant knight'. It is characteristic that the claims of these standard-bearers lay not in the sphere of religious merit but in that of chivalric experience and renown.

An inevitable corollary of the generalization of motivation which had occurred was a lack of interest in the nature of the enemy. After the lively interest displayed by Joinville in all the non-Christian individuals and groups whom he encountered in the East, the absence of curiosity shown by the author of the *Ldf* is remarkable. Quite simply, the *Sarrasins* were dogs, 'ugly and horrible'. Typically, the Turkish garrison captured at Rachowa in 1396 were all killed, an atrocity reciprocated by the Sultan a few weeks later. What looks like an astonishing reversion to the attitudes which had dominated at the time of the First Crusade is in one sense misleading, for much more was known in the late fourteenth century about the non-Christian world. There was also a good deal of curiosity among the literate public, as shown for example by the popularity of the travel book supposedly written by Sir John Mandeville, which made its appearance around the time of Boucicaut's birth. Its author's explanation for writing was that 'it is a long time past since there was any general passage over the sea into the Holy Land, and men covet to hear that land spoken of, and divers countries thereabout, and have of that great pleasure and enjoyment'.

Curiosity and toleration, however, were very different things. Mandeville's *Travels* opens with an appeal for the recovery of the Holy Land. 'Each good Christian man who is able, and has the means, should set himself to conquer our inheritance, and chase out therefrom those who are misbelievers.' Some contemporaries, such as the poet John Gower, did express concerns about the legitimacy of waging war against *Sarrasins* solely on the basis of their religion. In so doing they were carrying forward a 'liberal' tradition which in the thirteenth century had shaped papal policy, albeit not for very long. But such individuals lacked the influence of men like Boucicaut whose culture and personality committed them to an attitude of unflagging animosity, and who could muster the resources periodically to stoke up the fires of combat at the 'frontes guerrarum paganorum'. We shall never know the opinions of the population at large, but the hegemony of chivalric culture was such that it would be very rash to assume that any major inroads were made into the summary validation of attacks on non-Christians which is reflected so well by the *Ldf*.

Comparing Boucicaut with Joinville, Villehardouin, or the first Crusaders, the question is bound to arise whether crusading had become a mere adjunct of high aristocratic culture, one moreover which celebrated values of a predominantly worldly nature: honour, renown, splendour, even a brutal machismo. Yet Boucicaut and his friends certainly believed that they were fighting God's wars in all their conflicts with *Sarrasins*; and it is unacceptable for us to deny that they meant it unless we have supporting evidence. It is more helpful to view what occurred as proof of crusading's adaptability. One reason why it is so difficult to define crusading as a historical phenomenon is its chameleon-like ability to change as circumstances and society altered, in particular social values. The late fourteenth century was a period of extremes. In France above all, recurrent plague, social and political instability, and a worrying legacy of military defeats, helped to make the aristocracy unusually restless, keen to travel to strange places and go on pilgrimage, above all obsessed with proving and displaying their worth, individually and as a group. A series of truces with England enabled them to give more or less free rein to these characteristics, which expressed themselves most strikingly in warfare against unbelievers.

This was a phase, which eventually passed. To an observer in the very early years of the fifteenth century, it might well have seemed that crusading was coming to an end. After all, the Lithuanians were converted, Granada quiescent, the Ottoman Turks a spent force and the Mamluks far away. But twenty years later this scenario had already changed. The Turks had survived Tamerlane's career of destruction and were flexing their muscles again: in 1422 Sultan Murad II laid siege to Constantinople and in the following year he went to war with Venice. Meanwhile the emergence of the Hussite heresy in Bohemia and its entanglement with the political community there caused Pope Martin V, spiritual ruler of a newly unified Christendom, to declare a Crusade against the Hussites. A series of substantial preaching campaigns ensued against Hussites and Turks. An effective response to both enemies demanded the recruitment of armies rather than the services of freelance volunteers or groups, so the full apparatus of crusading vow, Cross and indulgence came to the fore. This was more than simply revival; once again it showed adaptability. For groups of individuals from two new, though very different backgrounds, Franciscan Observance and Italian humanism, evinced great admiration for crusading and became its most fervent advocates.

In these circumstances crusading, which had begun to look like an aristocratic preserve, showed that its social appeal could be as broad as it ever had been. In 1456 a Turkish siege of Belgrade was repulsed by a crusading army that was largely constituted of peasants recruited and led by the aged Fr Giovanni da Capistrano. Granted the events of 1456 were exceptional, and a recurrent lament in the following decades was that, for the most part, ordinary men and women no longer responded as their ancestors had to the summons to holy war. But the presence of the Crusade throughout fifteenth-century Europe, in the form of enthusiasts, theoreticians, envoys, preachers and collectors, remains indisputable. It is arguable that Boucicaut's generation helped make this possible through their wars against the *Sarrasins*, diffuse and incoherent though these sometimes seem in retrospect. These men formed a bridge between those Europeans for whom the Crusade had meant chiefly the defence or recovery of the Holy Land, and their descendants, for whom it entailed the defence of home and hearth against the Sultan's janissaries.

In fact it is very difficult to say when crusading did come to an end. Those parts of Europe which rejected Catholicism during the Reformation naturally turned their backs on an institution whose central features hinged on traditional beliefs and which was bound up with the papacy's authority. Yet the persistence of the Ottoman threat, up to the second siege of Vienna in 1683, meant that among the Catholic states which opposed them the practices as well as the habits and rhetoric of crusading enjoyed a remarkably protracted life. They were strongly in evidence, for example, at the battle of Lepanto in 1571, where Spanish, Venetian and papal galleys defeated the Turkish fleet. Crusading no longer stood for a broad-based movement, but in the Mediterranean lands it could still elicit enthusiasm and respect. A parallel can be found in the survival of the Order of St John. The Hospitallers successfully weathered all the storms of the fourteenth century, military, religious, political and financial. However, the Order's location on Rhodes made it extremely vulnerable to Turkish pressure during the fifteenth century and it seemed to have reached the end of its life when it was driven out of Rhodes in 1523 – at the same time as it was losing many of its northern European estates to the Protestants. In 1530, however, the Order was installed on Malta, which it defended heroically against Suleiman the Magnificent in 1565. Thereafter it carried on a war of licensed piracy against the Turks (the *corso*) for generations to come. The final decline of crusading, like the decay of the Order of St John, probably only set in during the late seventeenth and eighteenth centuries, when the Turks ceased to be a threat and a world-view shaped by religious belief was undermined by the European Enlightenment. But the question when the last Crusade occurred remains open, and with it that of who were the last Crusaders.

5

CONCLUSION:

CRUSADING AND CHRISTIANITY

I have used four texts from the history of the Crusades as windows into the motivation, thinking and behaviour of Crusaders from the First Crusade to the early fifteenth century. It is important now to try to draw together some of the main themes which have emerged from this process. Over the course of the three centuries which I have examined countless thousands of Catholics took the Cross to fight in a war which they believed was holy. The impact of their exertions on Christendom's relations with the Muslim and Orthodox worlds was immense. In both cases, and more particularly in the first, the Crusaders bequeathed a Black Legend (*legenda negra*) of brutality, greed and intolerance. No less important, though necessarily less dramatic, was the effect of crusading on European society. 'What was the effect of the Crusades on western civilisation? I simply don't know.' We have come a long way since Kenneth Clark's engaging admission of ignorance in *Civilisation* (1969). Thirty years on we can state with confidence that the many challenges posed by the decision to embark on a Crusade formed one of the greatest motors for innovation which existed in medieval Europe. Nothing could be more natural than our wish to understand the psychology of the people whose actions had effects that were so massive and so enduring.

At the same time few things are more difficult. In the first place, crusading was the collective result of thousands of individual decisions, each of which was by definition *sui generis*. Moreover, in the case of many of these decisions our possession of any evidence at all results from the fact that a big expedition occurred and was then written up, with all the possibilities for distortion which that brought with it. Hence the attractiveness of charter evidence, which for the most part was written down before the armies assembled and the many individual decisions were subsumed in the collective endeavour. Secondly, crusading was, again by definition, a transcendental exercise, one in which the participants believed that God had an active hand in what was taking place. When studying crusading we are not examining the rational. Travelling hundreds of miles to regain an empty tomb, or fighting for Jerusalem at Constantinople, in the Nile Delta or Tunisia, were not activities which we can place in the same category as, for example, building a village, engaging in a commercial venture or establishing a new tax. And thirdly, when we set aside these issues and simply address the surviving evidence, we face the problem that the character of crusading changed enormously in the course of its long existence. There is no ignoring the fact that a man like Marshal Boucicaut had different attitudes to those held by the armed pilgrims of the First Crusade. In the same way that a military balance sheet of crusading turns into a summary of the strengths and weaknesses of European armies generally, so any attempt to characterize crusading attitudes can become a *résumé* of how the religious thinking of the laity evolved between the eleventh and fourteenth centuries.

Despite all these problems one feels compelled to attempt a common characterization, and the main reason is the *legenda negra* referred to earlier. The most influential history of the Crusades written in the twentieth century was Sir Steven Runciman's three-volume account, and he concluded with a verdict of fierce moral denunciation.

'There was so much courage and so little honour, so much devotion and so little understanding. High ideals were besmirched by cruelty and greed, enterprise and endurance by a blind and narrow self-righteousness; and the Holy War itself was nothing more than a long act of intolerance in the name of God, which is the sin against the Holy Ghost.'

Runciman was primarily an historian of Byzantium, and his passage reflects the Orthodox viewpoint, itself derived largely from Byzantium's experience of the Fourth Crusade. But his verdict that crusading was unchristian is one which the contemporary Catholic Church has recently endorsed. As part of its celebration of the Jubilee Year, the Church's International Theological Commission issued a 12,000-word statement entitled 'Memory and Reconciliation: The Church and the Faults of the Past'. 'Memory and Reconciliation' was an investigation of how Catholics could engage in 'the purification of memory' called for by Pope John Paul II as one of the means by which they could benefit spiritually from the Jubilee Year in 2000. Essentially this entailed asking God's forgiveness for the sins that had been committed in his name in the past. And as the Pope had earlier put it:

> 'one painful chapter of history to which the sons and daughters
> of the Church must return with a spirit of repentance is that of
> the acquiescence given, especially in certain centuries, to intol-
> erance and even the use of violence in the service of truth'.

It was made clear in 'Memory and Reconciliation' that this included the Crusades. Irrespective of one's personal beliefs, 'Memory and Reconciliation' makes it all the more important to establish with, as much precision as possible, the Crusaders' own view of what they were doing.

It is essential to emphasize that crusading did not equate with the modern figure of speech in which it denotes altruistic or idealistic behaviour. This way of categorizing behaviour is essentially secular: a means of making moral judgements in a world in which religious belief has become a private matter. In medieval Europe moral judgements were exclusively based on religious values which were interpreted in a highly public way by the Church. One could even say that Crusaders were the reverse of altruistic since they took the Cross to guarantee their own salvation: recent research on the First Crusade, often viewed as the 'purest' in motivation, has stressed the over-whelming anxiety of people who took the Cross about what would happen when they died. It was more important to them than recovering Jerusalem, let alone assisting the Eastern Christians. Of course it would be perverse to argue that these people were being selfish: nobody could be blamed for wanting to avoid an eternity in hell, and the Church's mission was to help its flock achieve salvation. The Church's concern throughout was rather to ensure that those who took the Cross were acting from genuine devotion. It found clear expression right at the start, in the canon of the council of

34. Crusading knight of the thirteenth century. The conflation of military and religious values is seen at its most dramatic in the crosses which cover his surcoat and pennon.

Clermont regarding the Crusade: 'Whoever for devotion only, not to gain honour or money, goes to Jerusalem to liberate the Church of God can substitute this journey for all penance'. This concern with intention persisted throughout the preaching of the Crusades. The Church nurtured no illusions about the acquisitiveness of the knightly class, who from the beginning were targeted as the group most in need of forgiveness and possessing the military skills required for success. It was simply unrealistic to expect Crusaders not to show a lively interest in booty, relics, money, prisoners, and in some cases, land. The answer to the conundrum lay in distinguishing between behaviour and intention. It was expected that God would reward those who fought for him, but he would punish those who did so in the wrong spirit. Churchmen themselves were not saints and in some Crusade sermons they made overt use of the lure of such attractions, alongside such unpalatable devices as the atrocity story and incitement to vendetta. A conflation of the devotional and the secular occurred, and the realization that this had happened lay behind the anxiety displayed by Innocent III about the fate of the Fourth Crusade.

The search for pure motivation is therefore a fool's errand. At the same time most attempts to root crusading in economic causality have fallen foul of the evidence. Devotion is so prominent in the sources that it has to be given pride of place, properly contextualized in the development of family traditions, class solidarity and the demonstration of *prouesse*. There is no doubt that crusading did become entangled with two of medieval Europe's most dramatic processes of expansion and migration, the Iberian *Reconquista* and German movement into east-central Europe and the Baltic lands. But this was largely coincidental rather than causal, and in the eastern Mediterranean lands the failure to follow up conquest with effective settlement was one of the main reasons why the Crusades ultimately failed. It is reasonable enough to find crusading distasteful, but not to dismiss it as a materialistic wolf wearing a sheep's clothing of piety.

There were three central beliefs which were held by all Crusaders. The first was that their cause was unquestionably right. The charge that Crusaders were fanatics springs from this conviction, which flowed inevitably from their personal association with Christ's mission. As a form of imitation of Christ, crusading could no more be misguided or ethically wrong than Christ's death on the Cross could be. Hence the common descriptions of crusading as Christ's cause or concern (*causa Christi, negotium Christi*), of Crusaders as warriors of Christ (*milites Christi*), and of opponents as enemies of Christ or of the Cross (*inimici Christi, crucis*). This absolute sense of conviction did not always lead to the demonization of the enemy, as the example of Joinville shows, but it obviously removed any possibility of constructive dialogue. It set up barriers. It also heightened anxiety when diversions were mooted, most notably during the Fourth Crusade, for no greater crime could be imagined than betraying Christ's cause. In such circumstances it was the criteria of the 'Just War' to which Crusaders, above all their clerics, resorted in order to establish whether they should proceed or not. Indeed, it is hard to exaggerate the contribution made by 'Just War' ideas towards crusading apologetics. The approach laid down by St Augustine, though much refined since, not only established the nature of a just cause (*iusta causa*) but also addressed the other crucial features of any diversionary proposal, the possession of right intention (*intentio recta*) and the authority to sanction it.

The second central belief was the certainty of salvation. As the Provost of the Hospitallers put it when St Louis asked him for news of his brother Robert of Artois, who had been killed during his ill-advised charge into Mansurah, 'he was certain that his Majesty's brother was in paradise'. The respect accorded to those who died on Crusade meant that from the First Crusade onward there was a tendency to regard them as martyrs. Traditionally the Church had reserved this status for those who were executed while witnessing their faith. Applying it to Crusaders who died was bound to be problematic since so many perished in combat, when it was impossible to read their frame of mind with any accuracy; it was a different matter when they were killed in captivity, as after Nicopolis. The attitude of the Church therefore fluctuated. Joinville complained that St Louis should have been accorded the official status of martyr: 'for if Christ died on the Cross, why, so to speak did he, for it was as a Crusader wearing that holy sign that he passed away at Tunis'. The problem clearly was that this would have flooded the martyrologies with new names. But it was a hard argument to resist, especially when honouring the dead. In a powerful sermon preached on the anniversary of the battle of Mansurah in 1251, Cardinal Eudes of Châteauroux treated the dead Crusaders as martyrs. As such they enjoyed God's special company, described by one historian as 'a pleasing combination of knightly camaraderie and eucharistic conviviality'. This sort of chivalric Valhalla no doubt had considerable appeal to knights. But even without going so far, Crusade preachers naturally found the indulgence to be the most powerful weapon in their armoury. They communicated its meaning and scope with an imaginative repertoire of homely but effective metaphors.

The final belief held by all Crusaders was that the war they fought in was directly ordered by God, that 'God wills it' as they famously shouted in

1095 at Clermont. This is probably the most difficult conviction for us to grasp, because in the contemporary world it is associated with psychotic individuals like Charles Manson and socially alienated groups like the Branch Davidians at Waco. In the Middle Ages it was much more comprehensible due to the prevalence of an eschatological perception of history: if God was shaping all events then quite clearly he was capable of this most imperious form of intervention. There was nonetheless a significant difference between this and the other two beliefs. Personal association with Christ and the saving power of the Cross – mediated through his bride, the Church, flow quite naturally from New Testament theology and had numerous resonances in the Middle Ages. The idea of a divine mandate, by contrast, is rooted in Old Testament thinking relating to God's covenanted people and their role as a group in God's plan for his creation. The Crusaders considered themselves to be the New Israelites and the wars which they waged in the Holy Land to be the modern equivalents of the Old Testament conflicts. There are grounds for arguing that considered as a group experience, crusading was shaped as much by the Old Testament as by the New. Crusade sermons and chronicle accounts of expeditions were saturated in quotations from the Old Testament. Apart from rhetoric and justification, the precedent of the Israelites formed a reassuring and instructive parallel when defeats occurred. As in Old Testament times, God was clearly wrathful; but his support was not lost forever and it could be regained through public displays of penance. The difference was that the interpretation of God's purpose and will was now formalized in the Church, which had taken over a role exercised in the Old Testament by the prophets. Hence the anxiety expressed by the Church when charismatic figures attempted to revive the prophetic model, especially in the context of 'popular' Crusades with their tendency to acquire an agenda and momentum of their own. For due to its strong association with eschatology, crusading was from the start capable of unleashing dangerous currents of social unrest and anti-Semitic hatred.

It was of course the latter, together with the massacre in Jerusalem in 1099 and the sack of Constantinople in 1204, which gave rise to the Vatican's denunciation of crusading and its suggestion that Catholics should ask God for forgiveness. So was crusading fundamentally unchristian? From the perspective of today's Church, undoubtedly. But the theologians who wrote 'Memory and Reconciliation' made difficulties for themselves by admitting that people could only be judged by the standards of their times. As they put it:

'...an accurate historical judgement cannot prescind from careful study of the cultural conditioning of the times, as a result of which many people may have held in good faith that an authentic witness to the truth could include suppressing the opinions of others or at least paying no attention to them'.

This statement muddies the waters considerably, for if it applied to anything it applied to the Crusades. They received the support of European society in all regions and all levels during the centuries which we have been examining. This is not to deny that there were dissidents, especially among pacifist groups like the Waldensians. And repeated failure did erode for many the conviction of *deus vult*, as Humbert of Romans, a great Crusade preacher of the late thirteenth century, acknowledged. He referred to 'contradictors' (*oblocutores*) who argued that:

'...it is not in accordance with the Christian religion to shed blood in this way, even that of wicked infidels,' 'the Christian religion... ought to adhere to the example and teaching of Christ and the saints, (and) not initiate wars of any kind'.

However, in each generation such doubts tended to be buried by a resurgence of enthusiasm, and the overall degree of acceptance by contemporaries remains striking. As long as Catholics believed that the Holy Land should be in Christian hands it was hard to take issue with the argument that this could be achieved only by force, by whatever strategic means this was applied. Conversion, for example, simply did not exist as an alternative when the enemy was a Saladin or a Baybars.

There is a further problem with denouncing the Crusades as unchristian, which has become clear in recent years as we have built up much deeper knowledge of Crusade preaching and of the response to it. This is that the affective power, with which the Cross was preached, especially in the thirteenth century, places it within the mainstream of the great pastoral reform movement of the central Middle Ages. Painful though it is to accept, a movement which was responsible for terrible atrocities cannot be disentangled from one of the great spiritual revivals of the Christian past. Throughout its history the appeal of the crusading message to ordinary men and women resided very largely in the fact that it was in harmony with the dominant devotional impulses of the day. The First Crusade was an offspring of the practice of penitential pilgrimage, while also owing much to the networks of aristocratic patronage which embraced reformed Benedictine monasticism. Early crusading had strong links with the new theology of Christian love (*caritas*) which is usually associated with new orders such as the Cistercians, Premonstratensians and Austin canons. The powerful affinity between the mendicant friars and thirteenth-century crusading is increasingly obvious. And crusading continued to march in step with lay devotion in the late Middle Ages. It is thus difficult to condemn the Crusades without damning a good deal of the spiritual fabric of medieval Catholicism.

It is not hard to see why many people find the Crusades distressing, above all some of the visual images which it bequeathed in manuscript illumination: Christ personally leading Crusaders into action; an English knight fully accoutred for combat and sporting a tunic covered with crosses; or Christian and Muslim soldiers wrestling for possession of the relic of the True Cross. What shocks is the blending of the affective power of Christ's Cross, with all its connotations of willing suffering and sacrifice, with a forthright embrace of violence, carried out indeed at God's command. But if we are honest, we must accept that crusading was not only, by the standards of the time, a Christian practice, but also a thoroughly mainstream one. The more the Crusades are studied, the more apparent it becomes that they were an epitome of medieval life: this applies to their appeal, the way they were preached, their recruitment and organization, their military practices in the field, and the devotional life of the Crusaders. This is obvious once one grasps the central point that Crusaders were ordinary men and women who had undertaken an extraordinary commitment; to fulfil their vows they had to mobilize every material, social and political resource available to them. The answer for the Catholic who wants to respond positively to the Pope's challenge of 'purification of memory', and for non-Catholics who want to establish an ethical perspective on the crusading experience, must surely lie in precision: repudiating the massacres while celebrating the human achievement, in every sphere, to which the movement gave rise.

This means replacing the *legenda negra* of crusading with reality. As in every human activity there were Crusaders who were brutal, greedy, hypocritical and stupid, but to dismiss the entire movement in such terms is no more than a travesty. Nobody wants to return to the triumphalist view of crusading which characterized the older school of historiography, with its noble Christian paladins fighting treacherous Muslims. But replacing it with blanket denigration is no advance at all. The history of the Crusades is so astonishing that one need not fear that accuracy and objectivity will make the subject dull: its fascination is invincible. We have to let it work its own magic, which means stripping away myth of all kind and allowing the sources to tell their own story. When they do it becomes crystal clear that Islamic fears of a resurgence of crusading are without foundation, for it was the product of a society whose values, aspirations and anxieties have almost totally disappeared.

GLOSSARY

Byzantine empire   Successor state to the eastern lands of the Roman empire; in this period restricted to the Balkans and Asia Minor (Anatolia).

Franks   Inhabitants of Western Europe at the time of the First Crusade; also used to describe Europeans who settled in the Levant in the twelfth and thirteenth centuries.

Latin Christians   Adherents of the Catholic Church, particularly in terms of allegiance to the papacy.

Orthodox Christians   Adherents of the Greek Church

Reisen   Campaigns conducted into pagan Lithuania by the Teutonic Knights and volunteers from the West.

Shi'i Muslims   Muslims who believed that religious authority in Islam resided with the descendants of Muhammad's cousin and son-in-law, 'Ali; in this period represented in particular by the Fatimid caliphate at Cairo.

Sunni Muslims   Muslims who recognized the authority of the Abbasid caliphs based at Baghdad.

CHRONOLOGY

1095	27 November Pope Urban II proclaims the First Crusade at council of Clermont.
1096	May-June massacres of Jewish communities in Germany.
1097	1 July battle of Dorylaeum.
1098	3 June first Crusaders capture Antioch.
1099	15 July first Crusaders storm Jerusalem.
1119	27 June battle of the Field of Blood.
1124	7 July capture of Tyre by Franks and Venetian Crusaders.
1145	1 December Pope Eugenius III proclaims the Second Crusade
1187	4 July Saladin defeats King Guy of Lusignan at battle of Hattin.
1187	2 October Saladin takes Jerusalem.
1187	29 October Pope Gregory VIII proclaims the Third Crusade.
1198	Pope Innocent III proclaims the Fourth Crusade.
1202	24 November Crusaders take Zadar.
1203	17 July first capture of Constantinople by Crusaders.
1204	12 April second capture of Constantinople by Crusaders.
1212	'Children's Crusade'.
1217–29	Fifth Crusade.
1228–9	Crusade of the Emperor Frederick II.
1248	August Louis IX of France embarks for the East.
1250	February Louis IX's army defeated in Egypt.
1254	April Louis IX returns to France from Palestine.
1267	12 March Louis IX takes the Cross for the second time.
1270	25 August death of Louis IX in Tunisia.
1291	18 May Acre falls to Mamluks.
1312	Dissolution of the Order of the Knights Templar.
1365	10 October Peter I of Cyprus captures Alexandria.
1396	25 September battle of Nicopolis.
1399	Boucicaut's expedition to Constantinople.
1403	Boucicaut's raids on Turkish and Mamluk ports in the Levant.

SOME SUGGESTIONS FOR FURTHER READING

THE TEXTS

(Asterisked items are available in paperback)

Gesta Francorum et aliorum Hierosolimitanorum, ed. and trans. Rosalind Hill.
    (Oxford: Oxford University Press, 1972 and reprints)
Geoffrey of Villehardouin, *La Conquête de Constantinople*, ed. and trans. Edmond
    Faral. (Paris: *Société d'Édition Les Belles Lettres*, 1973)★
Jean de Joinville, *La Vie de saint Louis*, ed. and trans. Jacques Monfrin. (Paris:
    Dunod, 1995)
The best English translation of Villehardouin and Joinville is *Joinville and*
    Villehardouin: Chronicles of the Crusades, trans. M.R.B. Shaw.
    (Harmondsworth: Penguin Classics, 1962 and reprints)★
Le Livre des fais du bon messire Jehan le Maingre, dit Bouciquaut, mareschal de France
    et gouverneur de Jennes, ed. Denis Lalande. (Geneva: Droz, 1985)

SECONDARY WORKS

Jonathan Riley-Smith, ed., *The Oxford Illustrated History of the Crusades*. (Oxford:
    Oxford University Press, 1995)★
Jonathan Riley-Smith, *The Crusades: A Short History*. (London: Athlone, 1987)★
Norman Housley, *The Later Crusades, 1274–1580: From Lyons to Alcazar*.
    (Oxford: Oxford University Press, 1992)★
Carole Hillenbrand, *The Crusades: Islamic Perspectives*.
    (Edinburgh: Edinburgh University Press, 1999)★

LIST OF ILLUSTRATIONS AND MAPS

INDEX

The following abbreviations are used:

a archbishop [of]   k king [of]
b bishop [of]   p pope
c count [of]   q queen [of]
d duke [of]   s sultan [of]
e emperor [of]

All individuals are listed under their first name. Entries are given letter by letter.